The Gospel of Visitation

Dr. Hal and Rose Miller

© 2015 Dr. Hal and Rose Miller

All Rights Reserved.

No part of this publication may be reproduced, stored in a retrieval system, or transmitted, in any form or by any means, electronic, mechanical, photocopying, recording, or otherwise, without the written permission of the author.

First published by Dog Ear Publishing
4011 Vincennes Rd
Indianapolis, IN 46268
www.dogearpublishing.net

ISBN: 978-1-4575-4363-0

This book is printed on acid-free paper.

Printed in the United States of America

DEDICATION

The *Gospel of Visitation* is dedicated to Merle Denlinger, a woman whose love for God and his Word knew no bounds or limitations. She was a dedicated supporter of The Christ at the Door Ministry broadcasts, who shared the Good News with great fervor and lived it with great enthusiasm.

Contents

Meet the Authors v
Introduction 1
God's Plan of Visitation 9
At the Door Visitations 14
Five Famous Visitations 19
Voice Visitations 34
Artist Visitations 39
Dream Visitations 44
Near Death Visitations 55
Trance Visitations and other non-NDE Visitations 63
Disguise Visitations 72
Church Visitations 77
God Visitations 82
Visitations of the Living Word of God using the
    Written Word of God 90
Evil Visitations 97
The Steps of Opening our Door 104
The Steps of Discipleship 111
The Mind of Christ 121
The Visitations of Paul, Thomas Aquinas, Ramond Llull 128
Visitation and Nations 133
Visitation During Sickness 142
Conclusion 146

Hal Miller

The Flint Hills divide rolling Eastern Kansas from flat Western Kansas and extend from Manhattan, Kansas to Tulsa, Oklahoma. I was born on a small farm near Eureka, Kansas, just on the east side of the Flint Hills in 1929. I grew up during the great depression but living on a farm we had a garden, chickens, and cows for milk and butchered our own meat so we always had plenty to eat. No electricity, no indoor plumbing, no paved roads were a fact of life. Fritz, my Spitz dog, and I loved to roam the farm and Bachelor's Creek near the house. My younger sister, Lila, and I rode my bicycle to the one room school two miles away. My Aunt Esther gave me free piano lessons so I practiced the piano every day. In high school I played trombone in the band. When I was a junior in high school I realized I should start thinking about what I should do in life. I realized there were only two things I didn't want to do. Number one, I didn't want to be a doctor. I had been operated on for an inguinal hernia when I was too young to remember – except the experience left me with a fear of doctors. Number two, I didn't want to be a minister.

Although I attended the local Methodist Church with my grandmother, mother and sister every Sunday, I somehow got the idea that if we could all read the Bible, why did we need ministers to read the Bible for us? So as I mulled what to do in life the idea came to me that I should be a minister. This feeling, of course, was puzzling to me as I had no desire to be a minister. My desire was to be an airplane pilot, but my parents wouldn't sign so that I could join the navy air force after graduating from high school. I knew this minister feeling must be an impression from God, so I started praying about it and started reading the New Testament. I tentatively brought up the idea to my parents. My non-church-going father laughed at the idea that his son would want to be a minister. My mother counseled that you should have a divine call to be a successful minister. My musical aunt thought I could be of more use to humanity as a musician than as a minister. In the meantime I graduated from high school and Aunt Esther decided I should train to be a public school music teacher so she enrolled me at Wichita University. During the first semester I continued reading the New Testament and praying about my quandary. Why would someone who had no interest in being a minister have the feeling he should be a minister? It didn't make sense.

One night I read in the gospels "he that findeth his life shall lose it: and he that loseth his life for my sake shall find it." The Lord seemed to just lift that verse right off the page. My job wasn't to try to figure it out; my job was just to respond to the Lord's call. I finished the semester at Wichita University and then transferred to Baker University, a Methodist college and enrolled in the pre-ministry course. I stayed in a co-op house where we did our own cooking to lower costs and compared my experience with other pre-ministerial students I was living with. I had a problem. Since I did not feel at home in the church like the other pre-ministerial students did, I knew I would have to have a relationship with the Lord so He could guide me in how to minister His way. I read books on how to communicate with God. I continued praying.

At an Easter morning, I woke early and hiked to the edge of Baldwin City, Kansas and had a private sunrise service. The Lord spoke in an actual voice. He said, "You will have to seek beyond the church to know how to communicate with me." My soul was satisfied. I knew it was possible. I studied the sociologist Sorokin who pointed to revelation being as important as reason and science as a source of truth.

I graduated from Baker, and enrolled in Garrett Biblical seminary, a Methodist seminary in Evanston, IL. I was a youth pastor for I year in downtown Chicago near the Cook Co. school of nursing and the University of Illinois Medical School. I looked forward to the last seminary course on prayer. This must be when they teach the seminarians how to commune with God. But they didn't.

I was close to graduation and I still didn't have my contact with God to be able to be a minister. Then I remembered that he Lord said I would have to seek beyond the church to be able to know how to communicate with Him. Seminary wasn't beyond the church; it was a part of the church. I was in Chicago so there were many opportunities to seek beyond the church. The summer following graduation from college, I had attended a Fellowship of Reconciliation summer camp and met another camper who was the son of a chiropractor in Elkhart, IN. We continued our friendship after the FOR camp and as I attended seminary he occasionally visited on weekends. He told me that his father was a White Light radionics doctor and chiropractor who asked the Lord to direct his healing therapy. That sounded interesting – asking the Lord if it was His will that He would work with you to heal a patient. Would I like to accompany him for a weekend retreat at a location called The Garden Spot in Pennsylvania? Would I? You bet.

Dr. Leland Wood and his wife ran the retreat as well as taught in a local high school. In time the Lord worked through them to teach me how pray, be quiet and listen for the Lord to speak to me. My life-goal was on the way to being accomplished. In time I was invited to attend The Western Temple and also be taught by Dr. A. Stanley Rogers. I had gone to seminary to learn how to teach and preach; next the Lord instructed me to go to the National College of Chiropractic to be a healer for Him as well. I was the last of the thousand doctors who were taught to use white light radionics. After becoming established in chiropractic practice, the Lord instructed Dr. A. Stanley Rogers to help Dr. Leland Wood and me start broadcasting The Christ at the Door Ministry visitation message. We started broadcasting soon after Rose and I and our first two children survived the infamous 1965 Palm Sunday twin tornadoes that swept through northern Indiana. The Lord spared our lives. Rose was in the barn which was swept away around her. I just made it to the basement of our farm house with our first two children when the house was sucked away over our heads.

From 1959 to 2010, when I retired after 52 years of chiropractic practice, I was privileged to serve the Lord as a doctor of chiropractic and a radio minister; doing the exact two tasks I thought as a high school student I had no talents or desire to do. This book is a summary of the Christ at the Door radio broadcasts the Lord helped us prepare each week. We used a broadcast method in which Rose and I would talk about our subject and invite the radio listener to be a part of our conversation. The purpose of the broadcasts: To help the radio listener become aware that Jesus Christ really is at their door as He promises in Rev 3:20: "Behold I stand at the door and knock." Regardless of your faith and denomination, because Jesus Christ loves you, He personally visits and wants to have a living relationship with you.

Rose Miller

I was born in Pennsylvania during World War II. Some of my most frightening early childhood occurrences were the blackouts we had periodically, with a marshal going door to door to be sure all had their houses in the dark. I was three years old.

I was born with a love of God and country, a strong sense of law and order, and a great love of animals. Mom took me to see the movie, *Lassie Come Home* when I was four. She loved telling the story that during a particularly dramatic moment in Lassie's harrowing journey, I called out, "Don't worry Lassie; God will take care of you!" My parents were church-goers but eventually searched beyond that to find what they yearned for: a very close relationship with God and His Son. My parents met Dr. Rogers who shared his personal story and helped them start a retreat where they and others could pray and search how to have a more personal relationship with Divinity. I grew up knowing the Lord in a special and loving way. My goal would become to serve Him. It would be at our farm-retreat in Pennsylvania, The Garden Spot, where I later met my husband to be, Hal Miller.

When Hal and I married, we moved to Elkhart, Indiana where he began his chiropractic practice. I mourned leaving the farm and my animals in beautiful Pennsylvania and moving to a Midwestern town. My will and determination to serve the Lord was what saw me through this period of adjustment. If this was where we should be, then that was it, but I still desired country life. Fortunately, Hal did also, so before our second child was born we moved to a small farm in a near-by town. The devastating April 1965 tornados that swept the Midwest destroyed that dream, but God was merciful and started us upon a path that would be not only advantageous to us, but others as well.

Our new home would be New Acre Farm where Dad, Mom, my sister and her family could have homes together and also welcome others who wished to learn more about the path we had taken to find God and our Lord Jesus. My love of animals had never diminished and now was a chance for me to fulfill a childhood dream to raise horses.

This dream eventually allowed me to mentor several young girls. Sara had grown up in a bad part of town, and her parents were frequently in trouble with the law. However, her dad, in a moment of reasonableness, wanted to reward and encourage her good grades and brought her to the farm. She became one of my helpers, learned to ride, went to horse shows and even trained a young horse by herself. She did rise above her roots, went to college and got a good job, and helped her sister who wasn't as lucky in escaping as she was.

Shelby was a young girl bullied at school. She also became a horse enthusiast and the issues at school became trivial. Her life has been a testimony to her love of God.

Another young lady had no problems at home, but her parents thanked us for helping start their daughter on her path. She also not only became a wonderful horsewoman, but stayed in the animal field, becoming a vet technician.

Animals with their unconditional love can do more than humans in many proven cases. I have written books about my life with our many animals, and how I followed not only my dream, but God's will as it opened in my life (*The Horse That Wouldn't Trot*; *Mules, Mules and More Mules*, and *Little Miss Muffitt*).

As a part of the Christ at the Door Ministry, I became a speaker after my dad retired. This book along with the radio ministry messages has been Hal's research and work. I am blessed that I have had a part in sharing the good news that God wants to be a part of our lives. God speaks in many and mysterious ways. Not always in a voice, but known in your heart. Here is a recent experience I had.

In falling off one of my mules, I broke a vertebra in my lower back. It caused lots of pain, but I could walk. My biggest anguish wasn't the pain, but "why?" I pondered if it had happened because I wasn't to continue my work with animals. Was the Lord telling me something? It was the third in a close series of nasty mishaps. I was rattled.

Ever since I was a child of four, I knew I had a calling to work with animals, especially horses. In the elapsed time of thirty-plus years I had given up my animals twice: once to get married and again after the tornado. Both times God had blessed my return to loving and sharing my life with His creatures in an amazing way. Surely, He wouldn't be telling me to stop now.

Three days after my fall and still in great pain when standing or sitting, I was lying in bed watching television. I was also crying. The program was a Hallmark story, *Love Comes Softly*, about a young pioneer woman whose husband had died suddenly. She remarried and one day was sobbing and asking her new husband why God had let her husband die.

The man answered that God was like he was as a father to his own young daughter. He couldn't protect her from all pain, but he could be there for her as she went through it. God hadn't let her husband die.

I stopped crying and got still. Was God answering my question through a *television* show? I felt at peace and as I looked back through my life with animals, I was reminded how many, many times I had been through mishaps and been protected.

I knew in my heart, God had spoken, told me to dry my tears and "get on with the program." So be mindful of our blessed Lord in your life and the many wonderful ways He has of speaking to us. Many of the following stories of visitation are dramatic as well as inspiring, but remember: God speaks and leads in many every-day ways too; we must be heedful and keep our mind, heart, ears and eyes open.

INTRODUCTION

In 2003, G. Scott Sparrow, Ed. D., a spiritual mentor, psychotherapist, and writer wrote *Sacred Encounters with Jesus*. In 1995, Sparrow published *I Am with You Always: True Stories of Encounters with Jesus*. We recommend his books as a companion to this book, *The Gospel of Visitation*. What Sparrow calls "sacred encounters,"the Bible calls "visitations," two different terms for the same blessing. Dr. Sparrow asked Morton Kelsey, an Anglican charismatic and author of more than 20 books, to write the foreword for both books. Kelsey wrote:

> "*Sacred Encounters with Jesus* is a discerning and comprehensive account of how people still experience Christ today. What is surprising to me is that no one has previously taken the trouble to collect and explain the meaning of these experiences."

Unbeknown to both Kelsey and Sparrow, the *Christ at the Door Ministry*, a radio ministry, began broadcasting from a small town radio station, WKAM, in Goshen, IN, in 1965 proclaiming the same message: sacred encounters with Jesus still occur in our modern day and age. Our 15 minute broadcasts have continued on Christian radio stations since that time and have been aired on over 350 Christian stations, nationally and internationally. Our purpose is the same as Sparrow's: in contrast to those Christians who believe that once Christ came to earth, there will be no more visitations until his Second Coming, experience proves otherwise.

The *Gospel of Visitation* is a summary of the message our radio broadcasts have preached since 1965. It is the same message that Sparrow records in his books about Christ and Mary encounters. We both wish to call attention to the fact that the Lord still visits as He promises in Rev 3:20 "Behold, I stand at the door and knock: if any man hear my voice, and open the door, I will come in to him, and will sup with him, and he with me."

Since the *Christ at the Door Ministry* preaches the good news that in our modern day, the promise of Jesus that He is at our door to visit us is still true, it is only fitting that the *Christ at the Door Ministry* began as the result of a modern day visitation. The time: the 1920s. The place: Kansas City, Missouri. The person: a young attorney by the name of A. Stanley Rogers.

Stanley was born on a Missouri farm. As a boy his morning job was to "go fetch" the cows for milking. One summer morning he walked barefoot through the dew laden grass making footprints as he walked. He ambled down a grassy incline and was ready to walk up the other side toward the cows. But something happened. He was suddenly aware that a frame of time was missing. He remembered walking down the incline. But the next he remembered he was now on the other side of the incline. What happened to the time in-between? He saw his footprints on the far side and also where he was now standing. His feet had made an imprint clearly seen because of the dew in the grass. But there were no foot prints in the lower part of the incline between the two sides. He had been miraculously carried through the air from one side to the other side. Did this signify that the hand of God was on him at an early age?

Stanley was anxious to leave the farm and its hard manual work. After high school he made his way to Kansas City to make his fortune. He had a goal to escape the drudgery of farm work and become a millionaire. He worked at the Kansas City post office while he completed his education and became an attorney. He was a member of the Baptist Church in Kansas City, Missouri, where the minister wrote a book about the Second Coming of the Lord. He became a leader in the young people's organization and once organized a Baptist youth national assembly in Chicago. As he dated the secretaries of business leaders and looked at the books of their companies, which his dates could open for him secretly after business hours, he thought he found that their success formula was to borrow money at a low percent and be able to make a higher percent and become rich on the profit.

In addition to his practice as an attorney, Stanley began buying residential property with borrowed money and with his tenants' rent paid the mortgage and built up equity. Between his law practice and his real estate investments his accountants told him he was soon going to be a millionaire. His investment properties were so numerous that one day each month he took the time to personally inspect each property.

On one inspection day, Stanley was driving his expensive Marmon car when he had a Christ at the door experience. The Lord Jesus Christ appeared to Stanley by standing on the car's running board.

The Lord said, "I am going to take all of your wealth away from you."

"Why?"

"Because you have not kept my law of the tithe."

"That's old testament stuff," Stanley replied.

"No, I left the record that I came not to destroy the law, but to fulfill it."

"Well, you'll have a hell of a time doing it if you think you can take away all my wealth," Stanley flippantly replied to the Lord.

The Lord had delivered His message. He left, and Stanley continued his monthly inspection trip of his wealth.

What happened? The stock market crash of 1929 occurred. People couldn't pay their rent and Stanley's properties became vacant. He had to let the mortgage companies repossess all his properties. Soon he was not only broke, but also his wife left him when the luxurious living ceased. His health broke from the stress of financial loses and his diagnosis was stomach cancer. The Lord's prophecy was fulfilled. Because Stanley had not recognized that the Lord had blessed him and acknowledged the Lord's blessing by tithing, Stanley was now broken financially; his family was broken and his health was broken. The Lord didn't have "a hell of a time," it was Stanley who was having a "hell of a time."

David Wilkerson who wrote *The Cross and the Switchblade* often said, "I don't want a visitation. I want a habitation."

Stanley reflected how he had been carried through the air as a youth and how the Lord's words at His visitation became true. The Lord had taken all his wealth away. Stanley realized that "the gifts and calling of God are without repentance" (Rom 11:29). Jesus visited to rebuke his present life style and goals and visited to call him to follow Him. Stanley had been active in the church but did not have a personal relationship with Jesus. The Lord's visitation was His call to follow Him. Stanley knew that Jesus came to the door of his car and soon found that Rev 3:19 states, "As many as I love, I rebuke and chasten: be zealous therefore, and repent."

Stanley started working toward a re-visitation and habitation with the Lord. He began a life of prayer. He started reading his Bible. He forgot about his goal to be a millionaire and instead his goal was to take up his cross and follow the Lord. His goal was to be able to return to and feel the presence of the Lord. Stanley started repenting. After praying, he would be impressed to correct a sin he had committed. He was aided by a recurring dream. In the dream angels would come and examine his heart. They would say: "There is still some guilty stain on his heart." Stanley would wake up and be impressed that another sin needed correction or another action was needed to correct a wrong.

Finally after months of repenting and working to prepare to rightly come into the presence of the Lord and a re-visitation from the

Lord, Stanley lay down after lunch for a nap. He dreamed that an angel came and took him in his spiritual body to heaven. In heaven they arrived on the outside of a large amphitheater. When Stanley and the angel entered, Stanley could see that all seats were in a circle with aisles between the seats. All the aisles descended to a single table at the very bottom and center. At the table sat Jesus. In spite of all the people assembled that the Lord was teaching, Stanley rushed down an aisle to see Him. The Lord motioned for him to sit on a chair at the table. As Stanley looked at Jesus he absorbed so much love from Him that in tears of joy his heart expanded until the pressure against his chest wall caused him to faint. When he recovered from his faint Stanley found that he was resting his head on the Lord's breast. As he looked at Him again he felt so much love and cried so many tears of joy that he fainted again. Again he woke to find his head resting on the Lord's breast. After absorbing the Lord's love Stanley was finally able to remain conscious and through tears of joy asked if he could ask some questions about His will and plan. Jesus answered Stanley's questions, and the heavenly visitation completed, the angel escorted Stanley from the amphitheater, and back to his sleeping body. When Stanley woke from the dream, he found his shirt was wet from the tears of joy he had shed from feeling the love from the Lord by being in His spiritual presence.

One question Stanley asked was how he could maintain the Lord's presence for a daily walk with Him. The Lord said to pray the prayer found in Luke that he gave to his disciples to pray and the prayer would serve as a call to Him. He said he would add to the prayer to make it a modern day disciple's prayer. And if Stanley was serious in wanting a communing relationship he should pray three times a day (The Lord's Prayer, the prayer He prayed, is found in the 17th chapter of John). Later in his bible study Stanley found that in Psalm 55:17 David said; "Evening, and morning, and at noon, will I pray, and cry aloud: and he shall hear my voice." And Daniel also prayed three times a day (6:10).

In the process of repenting, Stanley of course also asked the Lord to heal his stomach cancer. Stanley's doctor search led him to a healing method called radionics, discovered by a Dr. Abrams, who by then was deceased. Stanley prayed and asked the Lord if He would spiritually use the material method of radionics to heal his cancer. The Lord guided Stanley to improve the earlier radionic machines and answered Stanley's prayer; his stomach cancer was healed without medication or surgery. Seeing the success of Stanley's healing, other doctors asked Stanley how to combine radionics with the power of prayer under the Lord's direction. This led Stanley to start teaching classes in what the doctors called the White Light Radionics healing method. During the depression doctors were struggling to make a living and the healing success of white light doctors soon became known. So during the depression Stanley always had a group of 33 doctors in training. By the end of the healing phase of his ministry, Stanley had taught a thousand doctors to be Christian healers for the Lord. He and his second wife maintained a retreat known as the 'Western Temple,' in the California mountains where doctors could come for worship, retreat, and for their own healing. Twice a year Stanley and his second wife personally visited the White Light doctors in training to assist in difficult cases and to also hold classes for new doctor training.

As the healing ministry was completed with the last of the thousand doctors trained, the Lord guided Stanley to recognize the power Satan had in controlling the physical universe. Stanley's spiritual work in resisting the Devil (James 4:7) was also helping prepare for the Second Coming of the Lord. Soon, the Lord directed the start of a radio ministry to announce that He was ending His thief in the night phase of visitation (1st Thes 5:2; 2nd Peter 3:10) and was now openly appearing to visit His children as the first step of His Second Coming. The first radio broadcast in 1965 was at a small station in a city that had a biblical connotation: Goshen, Indiana.

Why a ministry to emphasize that Jesus can openly be seen, felt, heard and experienced? As we read the Apostles' Creed, notice what the creed omits: "I believe in God, the Father Almighty, Creator of heaven and earth and in Jesus Christ, His only Son, our Lord: Who was conceived by the Holy Spirit, born of the Virgin Mary, suffered under Pontius Pilate, was crucified, died, and was buried. He descended into hell; the third day He arose from the dead; He ascended into heaven, sitteth at the right hand of God, the Father Almighty; from thence He shall come to judge the living and the dead. I believe in the Holy Spirit, the holy catholic Church, the communion of saints, the forgiveness of sins, the resurrection of the body, and life everlasting. Amen."

Note that there is no recognition of the fact that Jesus suffered the crucifixion to have the power to visit His own in the time period between His resurrection and His return at the Second Coming.

The Fundamental Creed does no better. This creed was published in a series of booklets between 1910 and 1915. This creed also shortchanges the Lord's power when it states: "The Bible is the inspired Word of God; that Jesus Christ was God in human flesh, was born of a virgin, lived a sinless life, died on the cross for the salvation of men and women, rose from the dead, ascended into heaven, and would return at the end of the age in great glory; that sin is real and not the product of fevered imaginations; that God's grace and not human effort is the source of salvation; and that the church is God's institution designed to build up Christians and to spread the gospel."

Again note that as in the Apostles' Creed the Fundamental Creed also has no recognition of the Lord's power to visit between ascending into heaven and returning at the end of the age. There is recognition of the Bible as the inspired written Word of God, but no recognition of Jesus Christ as the living Word of God. In fact too often the Bible is seen as our only way to know the Lord since the Lord is absent in human affairs. But the Bible clearly states: "Search the scriptures; for in them ye think ye have eternal life: and they are they which testify of me." (Jn 5:39). The written Word of God should lead us to the living Word of God. So often people have the attitude that their life is so insignificant the Lord can't be bothered to be concerned with their little life and their insignificant problems.

So our radio broadcasts and now this book is to help build the faith for you, the reader, that the Bible is true: Jesus Christ really is at your door as He promises in Revelation 3:20. There is fullness of joy in the presence of the Lord (Ps 16:11). When we invite Jesus through our door and into our lives, we (Jesus and His Father) will come unto him, and make our abode with him" (Jn 14:23). This is the habitation with the Lord that David Wilkerson prayed for. This is the goal of the Christ Encounters about which Sparrow wrote.

GOD'S PLAN OF VISITATION

Numbers 16:29: "...if they be visited after the visitation of all men..."

Chapter 16 of the book of Numbers tells the story of the rebellion of Korah, Dathan, Abiram and On against the leadership of Moses. Their complaint was that if all of the congregation was holy, why should Moses have more power than the rest of the congregation. To answer their complaint Moses used two tests: first, Moses knew that if they had received their visitation, the visitation of all men, they would have already understand God's plan for His people with his leadership and would not be complaining that God asked him to lead. Second, Moses knew that if these men would die the common death of all men then they would know his leadership was approved by God. They of course did not die a common death; the earth opened and they were swallowed up. Even though they knew that as a member of God's people, they were a holy congregation, they did not understand the fullness of God's plan because they had not yet received their individual visitation which all the congregation would receive. This verse tells us that God has a plan to visit all His creation in some way, at some time, at least once in their lifetime. And His visitation blesses us and instructs us in His plan for our lives.

Job 7:17 and 18 further explains God's plan of visitation. Job asks, "What is man, that thou shouldest magnify him? And that thou shouldest set thine heart upon him? And that thou shouldest visit him every morning, and try him every moment? Now we understand that God not only has a plan to visit man, but his original plan was to visit us daily. Genesis 3:8 confirms Job by telling us that Adam and Eve heard the "voice of the Lord God walking in the garden in the cool of the day." This was their daily visitation. God's plan for their life was given day by day. What a marvelous plan.

Job exclaims: "thy visitation hath preserved my spirit" (10:8). Job tells us his visitation: "I have heard of thee by the hearing of the ear: but now mine eye seeth thee" (42:5). Genesis and Job tell us that God meant to visit man daily. Revelation tells us that when the new heaven and new earth is created God will re-establish His original plan of the daily morning visitation. "Behold, the tabernacle of God is with men, and He will dwell with them, and they shall be His people, and God himself shall be with them, and be their God" (21:3). Visitation will be expanded to daily continuous fellowship. Hebrews further explains this future time of continuous visitation: "For this is the covenant that I will make with the house of Israel after those days, saith the Lord: I will put my laws into their mind, and write them in their heart; and I will be to them a God, and they shall be to me a people; And they shall not teach every man his neighbor, and every man his brother, saying, Know the Lord, for all shall know me, from the least to the greatest" (8:10,11). No priests, rabbis, preachers or teachers. God himself will instruct us.

Starting with God's first visitation to Adam and Eve through the Old Testament we have the record of God's past visitations to man. The psalmist asked: "O visit me with thy salvation" (106:4) and God did. We remember the Lord visited Abram when he was 99 (Gen. 17:1-22) and the Lord also visited Sarah (Gen 21:1). We remember Jacob's visitation at Bethel (Gen 28) when Jacob dreamed of the ladder reaching to heaven with angels ascending and descending and Jacob proclaimed "surely the Lord is in this place." We remember the visitation of Moses at the burning bush (Ex. 3:1-9) and at Mt. Sinai (33:11). Moses, Aaron, Nadab, Abihu and seventy of the elders of

Israel not only saw God but ate and drank in fellowship with God (Exodus 24:9-11). Ezekiel, Isaiah, Daniel and other prophets recorded their visitation experiences because "Out of heaven He made thee to hear His Voice, that He might instruct thee: and upon earth He shewed thee His great fire; and thou heardest His words out of the midst of the fire" (Deut 4:36).

The New Testament starts with the gospels detailing the visitation of Jesus Christ. Jesus foretold the destruction of Jerusalem because His people "knewest not the time of thy visitation" (Luke 19:44). Jesus taught that the Father's plan of visitation will continue even after His ministry on earth. Jesus said "My sheep hear my voice" (John 10:27). "He that is of God heareth God's words" (John 8:47). "Everyone that is of the truth heareth my voice" (John 18:37). "And this is the will of him that sent me, that every one which seeth the Son, and believeth on him, may have everlasting life" (John 6:40). The 14th chapter of John contains the promises of visitation three times. First Jesus promises: (v 18) "I will not leave you comfortless; I will come to you. Yet a little while, and the world seeth me no more; but ye see me: because I live ye shall live also."

The next promise of visitation is in verse 21 and again emphasizes that we can not only know Him; we can also see Him. "He that hath my commandments, and keepeth them, he it is that loveth me: and he that loveth me shall be loved of my Father, and I will love him, and will manifest myself to him." The third promise is that not only Jesus but also the Father will not only visit, but make their abode with the believer (v 23). "If a man love me, he will keep my words, and my Father will love him, and we will come unto him, and make our abode with him." We remember the Lord's visitation to His disciples after His ascension when He returned to visit them in the power of His resurrected body. We are familiar with Paul's visitation on the road to Damascus. God's plan of visitation continues to our present day because Hebrews admonishes: "See that ye refuse not Him that speaketh" (13:16).

A detailed promise of visitation is found in Revelation: "As many as I love, I rebuke and chasten; be zealous therefore, and repent. Behold, I stand at the door, and knock: if any man hear my voice, and open the door, I will come in to him, and will sup with him, and he with me. To him that overcometh will I grant to sit with me in my throne, even as I also overcame, and am set down with my Father in His throne" (3:19-21). We have too often limited this promise by saying that Jesus is at the door of our heart. But the New Testament promises include a bodily visitation.

The fact that visitations still occur in our modern day is reinforced by five polls. In 1986 George Gallup made a poll in response to a presidential candidate who claimed he was told by the Lord to run for president. Was such direct guidance from the Lord plausible? The poll found that 69 percent of the adults questioned said they had the experience of being led or guided by God in making a decision. Gallup found 36 percent of the adults he questioned had the experience of God speaking directly to them "through some means."

In 1987 a St. Cloud, MN Lutheran minister conducted a private poll of 2,000 members of 14 different Protestant and Catholic congregations. This minister had previously taught at a liberal denominational seminary that said miracles and direct guidance were folklore of the past but were not present in our modern day and age. His private poll found that 30 percent of those polled had either experienced a religious vision, a prophetic dream, heard a heavenly voice, or had a definite visitation experience. The liberal seminary was wrong.

In 1975 sociologist Andrew Greeley conducted a study for the National Opinion Research Center. The study asked the question: "Have you ever felt as though you were very close to a spiritual force that seemed to lift you out of yourself?" Thirty-five percent said yes. Of that 35 percent, 18 percent reported one or two experiences; 12 percent reported several experiences and 5 percent said they experienced such events often. Greeley also found in the study that the respondents who claimed to have entered these mystical states were in a state of psychological well-being substantially higher than the national average as measured by standard psychological scales.

Philip H. Wiebe grew up in a Mennonite household in Manitoba, Canada. While studying to obtain his Ph.D. in epistemology (the theory of knowledge and its validation) in the 1970s at the University of Adelaide in South Australia, he heard a professor of engineering from India relate his two visions of Jesus. A friend of his mother, a pastor, related seeing Jesus standing beside his mother while she was praying for a parishioner. These two experiences led to Wiebe placing advertisements by which he located thirty people who were willing to talk about their experience of Jesus visibly appearing to them. In *Visions of Jesus: Direct Encounters from the New Testament to Today* (1997, Oxford Press) Wiebe calls these experiences Christic visions and looks at different explanations to evaluate them. (Supernaturalistic, mentalistic and psychological, and neurophysiological) In 2014 Wiebe published the paperback *Visions and Appearances of Jesus* (Leafwood Publishers) where he expands the Christic experiences of the original thirty in his survey to also look at visitations during the New Testament times, ancient and medieval times, late medieval times and other modern visitation experiences.

Christians Chester and Lucille Hyssen in 1977 published *Visions of Jesus* which was republished in 1992 as *I Saw the Lord.* (Chosen Books) The experiences of Chicago area and other residents is another proof that God's plan to visit His own is still active.

AT THE DOOR VISITATIONS

Rev 3:20: "Behold, I stand at the door, and knock; if any man hear my voice, and open the door, I will come in to him, and will sup with him and he with me." Is this just a "figure of speech" or does Jesus actually visit by materially knocking at our door?

A housewife told us her experience of hearing an audible knock on her door. She went to the door, but no one was there. She went back to her housework thinking she was just hearing things. But she heard a second knock on her door. Again she went to the door, but again no one was there. She returned to her housework and a third time she heard a knock at the door. This time she quickly went to the door expecting to catch a child before the child had a chance to run away. But again, no one materially was at the door. She wondered what had happened. We explained God's plan of visitation can result in a physical experience of hearing an actual knock. We told her she could pray and ask for a second chance and invite the Lord into her life and home when she heard a knock materially at her door and no one was there that she could see materially.

Contrast this experience with another lady. She had been given just a few months to live because of her terminal cancer. Her nights were painful, so painful that her husband slept in a different room because her groans kept him awake. This night was especially painful and she was awake. She heard a knock at her front door. All her friends and neighbors used the rear door, so she was surprised to find no one materially present at the front door. But being familiar with Rev 3:20 she said out loud, "Lord, you're welcome in this home." She said she immediately felt a dramatic reduction in her pain, felt a peace, and was able to sleep the rest of the night.

These two experiences are witness to the truth that the Lord can actually knock materially at our door to see if we are willing to invite him into our lives. G. Scott Sparrow in *I Am with You Always: True Stories of Encounters with Jesus*, (1995, Bantam) gives two examples of people who rejected Christ when He came to their door:

> "A nurse told me that she dreamed she looked out of the window and saw the bright light of the rising sun and Jesus knocking on the emergency room door. Not wanting to face Him, she went up to the window and closed the blinds. I can still see the anguish in her face as she told me about this—her one and only Christ encounter. Another person intentionally sought an encounter with Christ, and thereafter dreamed that a basement door opened in her home and light poured out. She knew Christ was coming up the steps and would appear at any moment. She ran to the door and slammed it."

Sparrow asks: "How many of us are ready for such a meeting? Are we really ready to hear what this Being has to say to us?" (p 15) Romans 11:29: "The gifts and calling of God are without repentance." A visitation can bring the power to repent, but we miss that opportunity if we close the door when He knocks. If you have been visited by a material knock and had a similar experience of rejecting His Presence, you can pray for a second chance and invite the Lord into your home when he returns and promise to follow Him when he knocks again.

Sara Wood was a housewife living in Pennsylvania with her husband. One day she was startled to look up and see the Lord in the archway between the dining and living room. In time the Lord's presence gradually dissipated. She told her husband about seeing the Lord and they both wondered what it meant.

In time, Sara and her husband met the founder of the Christ at the Door Ministry as he was teaching a class on the Lord's method of healing to a group of doctors. When they told their experience the founder explained that the Lord was waiting for their invitation to invite Him into their home. After all, the Lord was knocking at an inside door of their home by physically appearing. What could they do at this late date? By prayer, they could invite Him to be a part of their home and by prayer ask for a second chance to have the blessing of seeing Him. After a season of prayer, the Lord reappeared at the interior door of their home at the same archway. Sara was alone when she saw the Lord appear again. This time she audibly thanked the Lord for His appearance and invited Him to be the King of their home. She said a smile appeared on his face as He was invited to stay.

There are other ways the Lord can come to our door. Some people have heard their name being called. One lady told us she had a "funny experience." She heard her name being called and she looked around but could see no person who would be calling her. Yet she heard her name called again and again. She remembered the experience because it was so unusual. She was not familiar with the story of Samuel and was not aware of God's plan to visit by knocking and calling our name. She did not know she could respond like Samuel: "Speak Lord, for thy servant heareth."

Another way the Lord can come to our door is to let us see a vision of Him – even a vision of Him knocking at our door. This was the experience of Marlene Thomas of Coulterville, IL in June, 1987. The *Sparta News-Plaindealer* carried the article of her experience. She was in her kitchen when her kitchen stove began making a ticking noise. This alarmed her as her range had previously exploded and caught fire. Because she was worried about another fire she prayed and asked God for help about the strange ticking. The stove didn't catch on fire, so she started setting the table. She looked at one of the placemats on the table and noticed this particular placemat looked different. At first she thought the placemat was just dirty, but when she looked closer she saw an image of Christ's head on the placemat. Just as soon as she recognized the image of Christ on the placemat, the kitchen stove stopped the strange ticking noise. Marlene called her mother's attention to the image of Christ and they both noticed that Christ's hand was visible and was ready to knock on a door. The image of Christ stayed on the placemat throughout the month of June, 1987 and many relatives and friends viewed the vision of Christ.

Images of Christ at the Door have been reported in the national media. The *Chicago Daily News* on Thursday, June 19, 1969 reported that in Port Neches, Texas, the 19-year-old adopted son of Mr. and Mrs. C.P. Bass saw the image of Jesus on the screen door of his parent's home. First the *Port Arthur News* and then the *Beaumont Enterprise* printed the story and it is estimated that 20,000 people came to view the image of Christ on the plastic screen door. What better way for the Lord to witness that he really is right at our door waiting for us to invite Him into our heart and into our daily lives.

On August 19, 1975 the *National Enquirer* carried the story of a four feet by two feet glowing image of Jesus Christ that began appearing May 18th on the wall of an abandoned mission school in Holman, New Mexico. The image began about 9 p.m. and continued until dawn every day. The sheriff of Mora County first scoffed at the early reports of the image but once he saw it, he started directing the traffic of those who came to see. It was clearly photographed by station *KOB-TV* in Albuquerque for their viewers.

In 1983 in Jasper, Alabama, the face of Jesus appeared on the door of a hospital patient who had been seriously injured. The father who had prayed for his son's recovery was facing the door when the vision suddenly appeared on April 9th. The father proclaimed the vision as a sign his son would recover.

On August 21, 1986 the *Associated Press* reported a vision of Christ appearing on a soybean oil storage tank in Fostoria, Ohio, a city 50 miles south of Toledo. The vision started about 5 or 6 p.m. and seemed to be formed by a combination of rust stains on the tank illuminated by sodium vapor lights. The news of the 3-D image resulted in so much traffic that four police officers were enlisted to direct the bumper to bumper traffic.

In Estill Springs, TN, in 1987, the face of Jesus appeared on the upright freezer door of Arlene Gardner just after dusk when a neighbor's bright porch light cast a mixture of light and shadow. Gardner said she believed the vision was a sign that Jesus is coming again soon. Two days after the vision appeared, Gardner had a dream in which Jesus explained how He connected her porch light to her freezer which turned her freezer into a "TV." She believed the Lord wanted His vision on television for the world to see. After the whole world had seen the Lord's face, she believed the vision would then go away. Gardner and her husband would witness to the crowd that would gather to see the vision every evening at dusk.

There continue to be reports of Christ appearing. In 2006 *Sun Magazine*, on March 20th, reported that Barry Opekokw of Meadow Lake, Canada, saw the Lord as a shimmering, hooded figure on his garage door. The image lingered for weeks and attracted hundreds of pilgrims. In another issue *SUN Magazine* reported that Mike Thompson of Cleveland, Ohio, found an image of Jesus on one of the pancakes he was preparing. For another report, Eve Alejandro-Pena of Oak Cliff, Texas, saw Our Lady of Guadalupe peering out of the bark of a tree in her yard. On the island of Cozumel it was reported that hundreds saw the image of Jesus appear on a beachside flowerpot in the wake of Hurricane Wilma, which had destroyed the island the year before. Fred Whan of Ontario, Canada, saw the face of Jesus on a burned fish cake in his kitchen. Another lady saw a vision of the Lord that appeared on the door to her bedroom.

These are just a few national press reports that we are aware of to remind us that Rev 3:20 contains the promise that Jesus really is at our door. He appears at the door in many different ways to emphasize that He is waiting for our invitation to invite Him through our door so He can commune with us and live with us daily.

VISITATION: FIVE FAMOUS VISATIONS

The basic Christian message is the gospel of salvation. Jesus by his life and death reconciled fallen man to God. And God provides in our day and age visits to His children to maintain our growth after we accept Jesus as our Lord and Savior. The Bible tells us that because of the resurrection, Jesus earned the right to return. And the gospels tell of the times Jesus returned to His disciples and promised to all of us, "lo, I am with you always, even unto the end of the world" (Mt 28:20). God's plan of visitation then is His direct action in our lives to maintain our salvation and to develop us in the fullness of faith.

The Christian religion is a result of God's interaction with His creation. His past interaction with men, women and children is a history (His story) we call the Bible. The Bible starts with a story of God's first visitations to the earth. After creating the earth, God created man and woman. Gen 3:8 tells us that Adam and Eve heard the voice of the Lord God walking in the garden in the cool of the day. God established His plan to visit His creation every morning. Job asks, "What is man, that thou shouldest magnify him? And that thou shouldest set thine heart upon him? And that thou shouldest visit him every morning, and try him every moment? (Job 7:17, 18). The Bible not only begins with God's plan to visit and instruct His creation, the Bible ends with that same promise. Revelation, the last book of the Bible, tells us that when the new heaven and new earth appear, "the tabernacle of God is with men, and He will dwell with them, and they shall be His people and God himself shall be with them, and be their God" (Rev 21:3). Hebrews gives this same promise that in the new covenant, "I will put my laws into their mind, and write them in their hearts: and I will be to them a God, and they shall be to me a people; And they shall not teach every man his neighbor, and every man his brother, saying, Know the Lord: for all shall know me, from the least to the greatest" (Heb 8:10, 11). God's original plan of daily visitation will continue.

Notice that God speaks twice; two scriptures tell us God's original plan was to visit us every morning; two scriptures tell us God's plan was to live with us every day so there is no need for preacher, priest or rabbi, for God will be present with man every day. Until that day, we all need to preach, teach and testify as we struggle to learn that there is a daily way to live with God through Jesus Christ His son and the Holy Spirit.

The basic Christian message is to envelop us in the fullness of faith. God, Jesus and the Holy Spirit have their direct access to us. If we are aware of this divine blessing we can drink the fullness thereof.

The visitation experiences of others will help you be aware of and ready for His visitations to you. Peter reminds us to "...be established in the present truth" (2nd Peter 1:12). The Bible tells God's past activity. We need to be aware of His present activity in our lives and in the lives of others. To be visited by God is a pearl of great price. By looking at the visitations of others, we can praise God for His intercession in the lives of those He loves. And as God touches earth we can learn more about Him with each visitation experience. And we can prepare for our visitation. Numbers (16:29) explains God's plan to visit all His creation. The book of Acts tells us that Jesus appeared for forty days after His resurrection before His final ascension when He was taken up and a cloud received Him out of their sight (Acts 1: 3,9). But as those assembled looked toward heaven as He ascended, two angels asked those assembled why they looked to heaven and watched His ascension. The angels reminded them that "this same Jesus, which is taken up from you into heaven, shall so come in like manner as ye have seen Him go into heaven" (Acts 1:11). In other words we should concentrate on His return instead of concentrating on His leaving. This verse usually is interpreted as reminding us to look for Jesus' return at His Second Coming. But it should also remind us to look for His return at any time. God visits us in dramatic ways as well as common ways. We want to review five dramatic visitations which have been widely reported in the media and therefore are widely known. We want to retell these famous visitations because they reinforce the fact that God still visits his own.

THE VISITATION OF DR. BUCKE

Richard Maurice Bucke was born in 1837, the seventh child of English parents who immigrated to Canada a year later. He graduated from McGill Medical School and set up a practice in Sarnia, Ontario in 1864. He soon was appointed Superintendent of two asylums for the insane in Hamilton and London, Ontario. In 1872 Buck was thirty-five, and in England on a visit. He and two friends had spent the evening in England reading from the poets Wadsworth, Shelley, Keats, Browning, and especially Whitman. He parted from his friends at midnight and was driving home in a horse-drawn carriage called a hansom. He said his mind was deeply under the influence of the ideas, images and emotions called up by the reading and conversation of the evening. He was calm and peaceful and in a state of quiet, almost passive enjoyment from enjoying the poets and their ideas. All at once and without warning of any kind, he found that he was wrapped around as it were by a flame-colored cloud. For an instant he thought the city was on fire; but just as quickly he knew that the fire, the light, was within himself. Directly he said there came upon him a sense of exultation, or immense joyousness accompanied and immediately followed by an intellectual illumination that was impossible for him to describe. He described the experience as a lightning flash of Brahmic splendor which lightened his life from that experience forward. The drop of Brahmic Bliss left an aftertaste of heaven with him. This visitation experience gave him immediate knowledge and insight; extended his mental energies and of course changed his life.

As a result of the visitation, Bucke wrote *Man's Moral Nature* (1879, G.P. Putnam & Sons) in which he examined the relationship between man's sympathetic nervous system and the moral nature of man. He wrote *Cosmic Consciousness* (1901) in which he developed the idea that there is a growing new cosmic consciousness; a mental evolution of mankind which he saw as lifting the whole of human life to a higher plane. The book is still re-published as "the classic investigation of the development of man's mystic relation to the infinite."

THE VISITATION OF DR. PETTI WAGNER

The visitation of Dr. Petti Wagner is recorded in her book *Murdered Heiress...Living Witness* (1984, Faith and Works, Inc.). Petti admits she was born with the proverbial silver spoon in her mouth. She was one of the heirs of the Peet fortune. Petti was not content to rely on the fortune she inherited. She was a successful business woman on her own terms. She accepted the Lord as a little girl in her Iowa church and accompanied her two children to church after her marriage. One Sunday as she knelt with her children she prayed, "God! I'm a hypocrite. I've listened to my children pray to You, but I can't talk to You like they can. Please give me their kind of faith – blind faith." Later, experiences would lead to her prayer being answered.

Petti was 56 in March 1971, when she was kidnapped and held in isolation in an abandoned hospital room in Houston, TX and beaten and poisoned by her captors hoping she would die so her captors could steal her considerable business and personal assets. Finally she was strapped down to an antiquated electroshock machine and given such a severe jolt of electricity that she had a near death experience. She could look down at her dead body as a brilliantly lit magnetic force propelled her through the universe. She was at peace in the light that surrounded her. Suddenly she saw a stunning glow and from this white glow a beautiful man appeared whom she recognized as Jesus Christ. Two chairs appeared and she and Jesus sat among the fleecy clouds and azure skies with an ethereal rose sheen around them. Petti was filled with a triumphant ecstasy as she and the Lord communicated without words. Finally the Lord asked, "Do you want to stay up here and work? Or do you want to go back to earth? Today you are the judge, not the jury. Any time there is an interruption in the blueprint of your life that the Heavenly Father has given you, you have a choice."

Petti felt an assurance that whatever her answer, the Lord could bring it to pass. Finally she responded, "My Lord, my work on earth is not done. I must wrap up many packages in red ribbons before my job is finished." Suddenly she was back in her electrocuted body. She prayed "God! Please help me! I cannot help myself."

The Lord responded in the same voice she heard in heaven: "I am the Lord your God. I am here to help you, not to hurt you. Do not be afraid. Keep a spoon tonight when they bring your supper tray, and I will help you escape."

Petti responded audibly: "Lord, whatever You say, whatever You want me to do, I'll say it. I'll do it."

Petti reminded the Lord she had been looking for a way of escape from her captors for ten whole days and if He could help her escape it would surely be a miracle.

The Lord responded: "As My creation, you are a miracle."

Petti looked at a time-and-temperature sign across the street and calculated that she had been without any earthly consciousness for approximately six hours. As the Lord laid out his plan for her escape, it didn't make any rational sense for Petti.

Knowing her thoughts, the Lord said, "As soon as you learn that I am not confined to logic, that I am supernatural and super-normal, we can work together. Let me show you who We are." Instantly a ball of light totally filled and illuminated the dingy room where Petti was confined. "We are One – Father, Son, and Holy Ghost," God announced. The bright orb split into three separate balls which formed a triangle.

Petti sensed that the shining spherical light at the top of the triangle was God the Father; Jesus was below and to the right and the Holy Spirit was below and to the left. Petti described the Father's voice as deep and booming with resonant overtones like nothing she had ever heard before. She described Jesus' voice as tender and compassionate, the same way He spoke in heaven. She described the voice of the Holy Spirit as somewhat like the nicest teacher she ever had.

Next Petti saw the three balls of light merge again into a single brilliant mass and God said, "Now we are One again."

She felt the presence of the visitation as not only light but also as pure love; she felt an arm enveloping and holding her. The light left her room but the Voices remained and taught her about God and also laid the groundwork for her escape. As they taught her about themselves, Petti said the Voices instructed her at times separately so she could recognize which phase of God was speaking and at other times they spoke together as one voice. That night she would escape by following their instruction. As the time for the escape plan approached, the Holy Spirit said, "Say this after Me – Lord, I'm one of Your little lost sheep. I've lost my way. Please take me back into the fold."

As Petti repeated the words she felt a rush of power come into her bruised and electrocuted body. This gave her super-human strength to remove screws from a Plexiglas panel over the windows with the spoon and allowed her to next remove the bars over the window. As Petti worked, she was interrupted several times to pray for a specific person by saying, "Father, forgive him. He knew not what he was doing." Petti recognized the names she was asked to pray for but she was puzzled why to pray. The Lord explained that when she found out what this person had done to harm her she would be angry and so the prayer for forgiveness was necessary to keep anger and bitterness and resentment and rebellion from entering her heart and becoming a hindrance to her life.

Finally with the Lord's direction and supernatural strength the window from her third-story window was opened. All she had to do was jump to the ground – but from the third floor. The Lord said: "Petti Wagner, walk out in faith as you have done all your life. Jump, and I will catch you! If you take the first step, I will take you by the hand every inch of the way. I did not make the water firm for Peter until he took the first step, nor did I save Isaac until Abraham lifted up the knife."

When Petti jumped, her body seemed almost weightless and she landed completely unhurt. When headlights of the first car came into view the Holy Spirit told her to hide in the ditch. A second car approached and the same instructions. But when the headlights of the third car appeared the Holy Spirit said, "This is a child of the Father. He will take you where you want to go."

The driver who picked her up said: "I could see you a long ways away. Why, just look at you. You have light all around you. You're lighting up the whole inside of my car." The driver took Petti to safety.

Petti began to put her life back together. The Holy Spirit began to come to her at three o'clock every morning to teach her the Bible. Because of her beatings she had trouble reading the small print of the Bible so the Holy Spirit would dictate verses to her. As she would write down what the Holy Spirit dictated, if she misspelled a word, He would stop her. "You must not write over that word, but draw a line through it. It represents one mistake you have made in your life. But remember, you can always start over. I have erased all your mistakes. I am restoring your soul."

Petti experienced miracles of healing as the Lord restored and healed her body. One day the Holy Spirit announced: "Today I am going to take away the terror forever." Petti looked up and saw the same bright ball of light enter her room, split momentarily into three smaller masses, and then the Father said, "I am the Lord thy God. I am here to help you and not to hurt you. Do not be afraid. We are all here – Father, Son, and Holy Spirit." Next God showed Petti the army of angels He had sent for her protection.

When Petti told the Lord, "I love you," she felt a sensation like the outpouring of liquid love which began warming her from the top of her head, spreading to the tips of her toes, and washing through every cell, inside and out. Next she saw the light radiance condense, diminish in size and stream away from her.

Because her business assets had been stolen by her captors, she needed an attorney. One day the Lord told her the name of the attorney to hire. She soon located the attorney. The Father, Son and Holy Spirit ministered to her from three o'clock to six o'clock every morning. She was taught spiritual truths and then shown how to minister these spiritual truths to others. They explained the basic doctrines about the three baptisms: 1. the born-again experience of being baptized into the Body of Christ by the Holy Spirit; 2. the baptism for repentance by immersion in water; 3. the baptism in the Holy Spirit, conducted by Jesus Himself as the Baptizer. They pointed her to the Scriptures about different subjects. When she was impressed to read Hebrews 9:14-19 she began to cover everything verbally with the blood of Jesus. A frequent verbal instruction to her was, "Petti, you take the first step, and I will lead you by the hand every step of the way."

As part of her recovery, Petti was directed to vacation in Acapulco which would be a healing for her nerves. In addition the Lord promised that she would meet the man of her life (she was divorced). She was directed to Las Brisas and to a large lighted cross shining over the city. She went to a little chapel by the cross and inside saw a full-sized statue of Jesus. As she gazed at the life-like nature of the statue of Jesus she heard the Heavenly Father say: "This is the Man of your life." As she cried and sobbed in joy she felt total cleansing, purified and healed and recognized that she belonged to the Man of her life – Jesus.

As she had not been a Christian before her abduction, she was learning fast from her directions direct from the Father, the Son and the Holy Spirit. In spite of her mountain-top experience and finding the Man of her life, one day she was despondent and told the Lord she felt her life was just about over. She suggested that God give what remained of her life to a seven-year-old boy sick with leukemia. The Lord answered, "It is not your life to give. You cannot run away from life, you cannot run away from death, you cannot run away from God, you cannot run away from yourself. I have these four walls built around you so high that you cannot climb over them. Now get up and fight."

God's words were a challenge. Petti took theology classes at Rice University, attended Bible studies, joined a church and gave her testimony to individuals she knew and later nationally through TV on the 700 Club as well as writing her book. The final testimony in her book: "I have seen God turn my calamities to good in so many ways."

We give thanks that her calamity which led to her near-death experience, her miraculous escape and healing and then her fellowship with God which continued has helped us be established in the present truth. We understand more about the Trinity. And we understand that in our modern day and age, God can still visit His own and can still perform miracles.

THE VISITATION OF BETTY BAXTER

Betty was raised in a Christian home and was converted when she was nine years old. At her conversion she had a vision of seeing her black heart. Next she saw an old rugged cross with the letters "He died for you," above the cross. Betty saw a big door in her black heart and saw Jesus come to the door and listen to her heart. Jesus knocked and listened; a second time Jesus knocked and listened. The third time Jesus knocked Betty saw the door fly open and Jesus walked in. Betty in her vision knew that Jesus had entered her heart and He had removed the sin and blackness.

Two years later, at age 11, Betty had to quit the fifth grade because of her scoliosis, heart and kidney disease. Her father took her to the University Hospital in Minneapolis, Minnesota, when Betty was 13 because she had developed St. Vitus Dance. The hospital could only give her morphine for her pain and send her home to die. Betty had another visitation. Jesus came to her door and called her name softy three times. After her third call Betty answered and said, "Yes Lord, stay and talk with me for a little while because I am so lonesome." This began continuing visitations when the Lord would visit her. Many times the Lord would say, "Betty, I love you."

By age 15 Betty's physical condition deteriorated further. Large knots formed in her scoliosis. Her arms were paralyzed from her shoulders to her wrists and her head was twisted and turned toward her chest. Her pain increased and she would go blind for weeks at a time; she would become deaf for weeks and unable to speak for weeks. As her body deteriorated more, she lapsed into unconsciousness for four days and four nights. But as she was dying, she had a near death experience. She could see herself going through the valley of death. But suddenly in the darkness of the valley of death, the Lord appeared and took her hand in His hand and they walked toward the river which separated them from heaven. Instead of accompanying Betty into the City of God, the Lord said to Betty in a soft kind voice, "No, Betty, it's not your time to cross yet. Go back and fulfill the call I gave you when you were nine years old. Go back for you are going to have healing in the fall."

Betty regained consciousness and on the 14th of August her speech returned. But the knots on her scoliosis were growing larger. Betty prayed and told the Lord that her pain was so bad that she wondered if the Lord would call August "fall," and come and heal her. She promised that if the Lord healed her she would serve Him the rest of her life. The Lord spoke to her. "I am going to heal you completely August 24th, Sunday afternoon at 3:00."

Soon Betty's mother came into her room and said the Lord had spoken inwardly to her and said, "I have heard your prayers and I am going to reward you for your faithfulness. I am going to heal Betty, August 24th, Sunday afternoon at 3:00."

On the appointed day at 10 minutes to 3:00, Betty, her mother, and a few friends began praying and praising God. Betty became lost in the spirit of God. She saw before her two rows of trees, standing tall and straight. She saw one of the trees begin to bend until the tip of the tree touched the ground. She wondered why this one tree was all bent over. Next, she saw the Lord coming down the rows of trees toward her. This gave her a thrill as it always did when she saw Jesus. She saw Jesus approach the bent tree. Jesus smiled at Betty and then the Lord placed his hand on the bent tree and with a loud crack and pop the tree became straight. Betty said to herself, "That's me all right. He will touch my body and the bones will crack and pop and I will stand up straight and be well."

Next Betty heard a great voice which reminded her of a storm coming up fast. She heard the wind as it roared. Betty tried to speak above the roar of the wind. "He's coming; don't you hear Him? He's come at last." The wind and noise subsided suddenly and it was calm and quiet. Betty knew that in this quietness Jesus would come. As she sat in her big chair all at once she saw a great white fleecy cloud, and out of the cloud stepped Jesus. She knew it wasn't a vision; it wasn't a dream; it was Jesus. As Jesus walked toward her, tall and broad in his glistening white robe she noted his brown hair was parted in the middle and it fell over his shoulders in soft waves. But she was drawn to his eyes. As Jesus drew closer, he outstretched his arms toward her. She could see the ugly prints of the nails in His hands. She felt small and unworthy. The closer Jesus came, the better Betty felt. Jesus smiled at her and she wasn't afraid anymore. She maintained her gaze into Jesus eyes which were filled with beauty and compassion.

Jesus came closer and finally He was standing at the side of Betty's chair. One part of His garment was loose and it fell inside her chair and if her arms had not been paralyzed she could have touched His garment. Jesus leaned down and spoke, "Betty, you have been patient, kind and loving. I am going to promise you health, joy and happiness."

She saw Jesus reach out his hand and place it on the very center of her spine on one of the large knots. A feeling as hot as fire surged through her entire body. With His two hands, Jesus took her head and squeezed it. When Jesus let go, Betty could breathe normally and she knew her head was normal. Next she felt His hot hands rub over the organs of her stomach and she knew her kidney and all her internal organs were healed. Next Jesus placed His hands on her spine again and she felt a tingling sensation like she had touched a live electric wire and felt an electrical current charge through her.

She estimates Jesus healed her body in ten seconds. She immediately got up and stood straight. She maintained her eye contact with the Lord and He said, "Betty, I am giving you the desire of your heart to be healed. You are normal and well. You have health now. You are completely well because I healed you." After a pause the Lord concluded, "Now remember, every day look at the clouds and watch. The next time you see me coming in a cloud, I will not leave you here but I will take you to be with me forever."

Betty was fifteen. Betty gave her witness at many evangelistic campaigns and she continued to give her testimony as she promised. She published her story in a 1971 pamphlet titled *"The Betty Baxter Story, a miracle of healing as told by herself."* Betty's visitation gives us faith that God still continues His plan of visitation and can still perform miracles.

THE VISITATION OF VIRGINIA LIVELY

The fourth well-known visitation was written in the August, 1966 issue of *Guidepost* magazine. Her witness was titled: *"Three Months in His Presence."* At the time of her visitation Virginia was a Florida housewife who was married and had two children. She described herself as a typical civic-minded church-goer. In October she had been in charge of a Halloween Carnival for the local PTA. As she was riding home with her husband from a PTA meeting she began to cry because of the effects of the criticism she had received of her plans for the carnival. She cried herself to sleep that night and cried all the next day. In fact she cried for four days and was sure she was having a nervous breakdown.

On the fourth day Virginia said a curious change took place in her life. All at once there seemed to be a power in the air around her in the living room of her home. The atmosphere seemed to hum and crackle as though she was standing in the center of a vast electric storm. Virginia sat down in her living room and looked through the picture window toward the eastern horizon. She saw a ball of light appear on the horizon where the earth and sky came together. She watched as this ball of light came rushing toward her at incredible speed. She could see that the ball was white but all the colors of the rainbow seemed to pour from it. She watched as the ball of light came into her living room and took a position at her right shoulder. Next from the light there emerged a face. She realized that the face was Jesus and He was smiling at her.

She described the Lord as "the most beautiful countenance I have ever seen." Her first thought was, "He is perfect." She marveled at the color of His eyes, at the power and freedom His presence brought. Virginia was struck by two things. First was the Lord's humor; at times he would break out in outright laughter. Second was His utter lack of condemnation. She felt the absolute caring, unconditional love that radiated from His eyes. Being in His Presence brought ecstasy to Virginia. And this ecstasy by the presence of the Lord stayed with Virginia for three months. His face and His presence brought a joy to her life she had never known before. She couldn't read enough of the Bible. She said reading the Bible "was like tearing open a letter from someone who had known this Presence as a flesh and blood person, full of just the kind of specific details I longed to hear."

After three months, the face of Jesus left, but when He removed His face He told Virginia, "I will always be with you." Virginia's visitation which lasted three months gives us faith that His plan of visitation is still active in our day and age.

THE VISITATIONS OF DAVID E. TAYLOR

David records his visitation experiences in *Face to Face Appearances from Jesus: The Ultimate Intimacy* (2009, Destiny Image). David was a typical unsaved teenager, "smoking dope, marijuana, using bad language and cursing, partying, and having premarital sex. I was even involved with gangs and hung around cocaine-dealing drug lords" (p 23).

But the Lord appeared before David while he was asleep in 1989 and called him, saying, "David, forsake your best friend, give your life to Me, and follow Me" (p 22). David responded to the Lord's call and his book tells how he grew in his relationship with the Lord until the Lord could call him "friend" and even take him to heaven. He said of his first book, "The purpose that the Lord gave me for writing this book as your brother in Christ was not to flaunt and pridefully boast of my supernatural experiences with the Lord…He told me that His purpose for this book was to be a witness of these things which I have seen and heard from Him on a face-to-face level to build faith in your life and to let you know that you too can have this face-to-face relationship with God's Son" (p 11). He explains that "a visitation does not necessarily have to be an appearance from the Lord, but an appearance from the Lord is a visitation. In this book, we are talking about face-to-face appearance visitations. All appearances from the Lord are not necessarily face-to-face appearances" (p 246). So David worked that his visitation became a habitation, continuing appearances.

In *I Am with You Always: True Stories of Encounters with Jesus*, G. Scott Sparrow, Ed.D., explains the significance of hearing and learning from the visitation experiences of others: "Each of us might ask, what do these experiences mean to me? What am I called to do?

These are difficult questions. But the evidence provided by the Christ encounters strongly suggests one answer: Jesus manifests to call us into a closer relationship with Him or with our own deepest potentials. And He seems to expect for us to strive to remain in constant relationship, or communion, with Him or our spiritual calling" (p 217).

In amplifying and underscoring Sparrow's reasons, David E. Taylor notes the following reasons the Bible gives for the Lord appearing to us: (p 239-246) because we diligently seek Him; to call us as His ministers and servants; to make us a witness; so that we can become like He is; to preserve our lives; to bring the help of God; a sign of the Lord's favor; to reveal the knowledge of the glory of His Father; to disclose to us visibly who He is; to comfort us; to confirm and make authentic our apostolic call; to show Himself alive and risen from the dead; to show us and release upon us many infallible proofs, signs, wonders, and miracles that have never been seen; to bring salvation to our lives; to answer our prayer requests; to build His Church and saints; to release rewards, blessings, positions of authority, and eternal crowns to us; to inspect us; to bring the message that His Father is the Head of the Church; to lead and guide us where to go geographically; to correct us, and to cleanse and refine us.

In 2011 David wrote a sequel to his first book titled *My trip to Heaven: Face to Face with Jesus*. In this book the Lord explains: (p 172) "There's a difference in My kingdom with those who love me. Everyone who is a believer is not necessarily part of the elect or married to Me in this level of union. There is a difference in relationship levels with Me. I will be as close and intimate as you will allow Me to be."

We recommend both Sparrow's and Taylor's books to also build your faith that Jesus Christ really is at your door.

VOICE VISITATIONS

Psalm 65:9 "Thou visitest the earth." Psalm 106:4 "O visit me with thy salvation." Psalm 17:3 "Thou hast visited me in the night." Psalm 8:4 "What is man, that Thou art mindful of him? And the son of man, that Thou visitest him?"

The most dramatic visitation is a sight visitation; a visitation when we see the Lord. The Lord lets us use our physical sense of sight to be aware of His Presence. But we can be aware of His Presence in other ways. For example Jesus in Rev. 3:20 states, "If any man hear my voice and open the door, I will come in to him..." Many people have heard the Lord speak to them. These voice visitations can be either an outer and audible voice we hear with our ears or an inner voice that we hear in our mind.

We are familiar with the Old Testament voice visitation of Samuel (1 Samuel, chap. 3). We remember that Samuel was a boy who ministered unto the Lord before Eli the high priest. Samuel heard a voice calling him by name. Samuel thought the voice he heard came from Eli, so he ran to Eli and said, "Here am I, for thou didst call me." But of course Eli had not called so he told the boy Samuel to go back to sleep. When the same thing happened a third time the high priest realized it was the Lord who was calling Samuel, so Eli told the boy that if the Lord called again to respond to the Lord by saying, "Speak, for thy servant heareth."

The scriptures tell us that the Lord did speak a fourth time only this time "...the Lord came and stood and called as at other times." This time Samuel responded and the Lord gave Samuel a message to take to the high priest Eli." Revelation 3:20 says, "...if any man hear my voice, and open the door, I will come into him." Samuel heard the Lord; responded, and followed the Lord's instruction. Samuel continued his face to face relationship with the Lord. The message for us is the same: If we hear the Lord calling us, we should acknowledge the voice of the Lord by responding and invite the Lord to give us any instruction He wishes.

A New Testament audible voice visitation we are familiar with is the call of Saul on the road to Damascus (Acts 9). Saul heard the Lord saying unto him, "Saul, Saul, why persecutest thou me?" Note the interchange between Saul and the Lord. First Saul asked, "Who art thou, Lord?" And the Lord answered, "I am Jesus whom thou persecutes; it is hard for thee to kick against the pricks." Next, notice how similar Saul's response was to the boy Samuel's response. Saul asked, "Lord, what wilt Thou have me to do?" And the Lord told Saul exactly what "thou must do." And the power of the presence of the Lord changed Saul from a persecutor of Christians to a missionary for Christ because, like Samuel, Saul responded and followed the instructions given by the Lord at the visitation. Many have noted that you are never the same after a visitation because the Lord's power with the visitation changes us into a new person – if we recognize the Lord calling us and if we respond to His instructions.

A Christian widow shared her audible voice visitation. She had adjusted to life alone after her husband passed. A new man was showing interest in her. Being a Christian, she prayed and asked if it was His will for her to remarry. She prayed daily and one day the Lord said audibly, "There is another woman involved." She knew she didn't want to waste her time knowing he was just "playing the field."

What thing is hard for the Lord? He really is right at our door.

We remember the famous Kansas runner, Jim Ryun. The Associated Press on April 15, 1986, called Ryun the world's best middle-distance runner between 1966 and 1975 because Ryun had set world records for the half-mile, 1,500 meters and the mile. He was the first high school runner to break four minutes running the mile and was a three-time Olympian. Ryun, a born-again Christian, explained why he retired in 1976. "God spoke to me, saying, 'You fought a good fight, you ran a good race, but now you're finished.'" What a way to retire. After retirement Ryan ran for fun, wrote his book *In Quest of Glory* and gave inspiring talks to youngsters.

On Feb. 7, 1972, a Christian school teacher, Mrs. G, was on her way to work. Was she ready to retire? Did she want to retire? These questions had been on her mind. This morning the Lord appeared to her as she was driving her car and told her to retire at the end of that school year. What a way to retire. She was privileged to have the Lord appear and also speak to her that it was His will for her to retire. Like Ryun this Christian lady was receiving her reward of "Well done, good and faithful servant" (Matt 25:21).

Guidepost magazine has reported many voice visitation experiences and continues reporting these experiences. In addition to hearing the audible voice of the Lord, the Lord can also speak mind to mind in a voice heard inwardly. On July 19, 1981, the Associated Press reported an inner voice visitation. Jean and Robert Sternecker were at the Kansas City, MO Hyatt popular Friday night tea dance. They were sitting directly beneath the skywalks that would later collapse and kill 111 people and injure 180 more. As they were listening to Duke Ellington's orchestra, Mrs. Sternecker said she felt an eeriness in the air which diverted her attention. She said, "The best way I can describe it is to say a voice came over me, saying 'Run, Jean, run.' It was inside me, but it was commanding." And it saved her and her husband's life. They were Christians able to be impressed by the Lord by His voice speaking inwardly just as real as if He had spoken outwardly.

For another inner voice visitation, we relate the experience of Leland Wood when he was six years old. He was playing in a boat with two other boys in the state of Pennsylvania. The boys didn't notice that the boat had floated away from the shore and into the deep water in the middle of the pond. Neither did any of the boys notice that the boat was leaking and collecting water fast. When they finally noticed, they tried to get the boat back to shore but in their haste they overturned it. None of the boys could swim. As Leland sank under water the Lord spoke to him and told him not to be afraid. The Lord said when he came back to the surface, to just take hold of the boat. With the Lord's inner words came a feeling of contentment and peace. Instead of being terrified and afraid of drowning, Leland remembers he was smiling. When he surfaced, he found that the boat had overturned again and was floating. He took hold of the boat and soon the other boys did the same as they came to the surface. Leland said he heard the voice of the Lord through his ears just as surely as anyone would speak audibly to him. Praise the Lord for His plan of visitation.

For another inner voice visitation let's relate the experience of a 10-year-old girl, Rose Wood. She was swinging in her swing and heard her voice being called: "Rose." She heard the inner voice again, and then again. Three times. The experience was so remarkable that she remembered it. Not knowing what it meant, when she met the founder of the Christ at the Door Ministry, he explained that this was her calling, just as the boy Samuel was called. She could, at this late date, still answer, "Lord, speak, for thy servant heareth." By prayer she responded and the Lord did respond and guided and blessed her life.

Author Paula Rinehart has written a series of books titled *Sex and the Soul of a Woman* but with different sub-titles. In her book subtitled *"How God Restores the Beauty of Relationship from the Pain of Regret"* (2010, Zondervan), Paula tells the story of Lynn's heartache from her earlier sexual promiscuity before she gave her life to Christ in her late twenties. After other dating disappointments Lynn was now 35. She met Jeff and they began courting. Lynn tells her visitation experience: (p 168) "She remembers praying one morning early in their courting and words formed in her brain as clear as though she had heard them out loud: <u>DO...NOT...SLEEP...WITH...THIS...MAN.</u>" God could not have made it clearer to her that this relationship was to be different from the others. She and Jeff made a vow together to wait until they were married to sleep together. They followed God's direct inner voice to Lynn and God blessed their marriage.

"If any man hear my voice, and open the door..."

ARTIST VISITATIONS

How do we know what Jesus looks like? If we want a portrait of ourselves, we would go to a portrait painter, and we would sit while the artist painted our features on the canvas. Or if we wanted to send our picture to a friend who wanted to know what we look like, we would simply use a camera to take our picture. The Lord has used both of these ways so we can know what He looks like.

Charles Sindelar was a young artist who was living on the west coast before World War II. He was married, and one day his wife noticed a sudden change in her husband's behavior. She sensed something was bothering him. After a great deal of coaxing Charles finally admitted he was worried that he was soon going to die. "I've been waking up from a sound sleep about 2:00 every night and I see the Lord. I've heard that if the Lord appears to you, he is coming to take you to heaven at your death. I am afraid I will die."

Sindelar's wife knew a friend who had the gift the apostle Paul spoke of as the gift of discerning spirit. His wife wondered if this friend could shed some light on his experience. She and her husband told their Christian friend about his recurrent dream. They told about Charles experience of waking up every night at 2:00 and seeing the Lord. When Charles said he was afraid of soon dying, the Christian lady couldn't help but laugh. Charles didn't see anything funny about his experience and wanted to know what the Christian lady thought was so funny.

She explained, "You are an artist. The Lord wants you to paint His portrait. He is coming to sit for you just as you ask a client to make a series of appointments to sit as you paint their portrait. Tonight when He wakes you up, go to your studio and paint His portrait."

Sindelar's studio was in his home, so sure enough, that night the Lord again woke Sindelar at 2:00 a.m. He dressed, went to his studio and the Lord sat for an hour while His portrait was started. After an hour, Sindelar returned to bed and the next night the Lord again woke the artist up at 2:00 a.m. These 2:00 a.m. visits continued until Sindelar completed the portrait of the Lord. He titled the face of Christ that he painted "Peace be with you on this day." This title probably represents the peace that Sindelar felt in his own life after his fear of death was replaced with the power of the presence of the Lord he absorbed as he painted the Lord's portrait.

Jesus tells us in Rev. 3:20, "Behold, I stand at the door and knock." A famous picture by the artist Warner Sallman shows the Lord doing just as the Bible promises: Jesus is knocking at a door, hence Sallman's title: *At the Door*. The story behind the painting can be an inspiration to us because it is the story of the inspiration that Sallman also experienced. Warner Sallman came from a Christian home and early in life he enjoyed the pictures that artists painted to illustrate the Bible events. The Bible illustrations of Gustav Dore especially stimulated his desire to become a Christian artist. He apprenticed in an art studio at the age of fourteen and later studied art at the Chicago Art Institute. At the same time he took classes at a Bible Institute. He was married in 1916 when he was 24 years old. A year later in 1917, Sallman's doctor discovered he had TB of the lymph glands and gave Warner only three months to live if he didn't have immediate surgery to remove the tuberculosis lymph glands. Sallman and his wife prayed about the diagnosis and decided to do all they could to serve God in the three months he had left to live. He continued to treat the TB but didn't feel led by the Lord to have the surgery the doctor recommended. When his pain was gone at the end of three months and he was still alive, Warner and his wife knew the Lord had healed him of tuberculosis.

Several years later at the age of thirty-one, after his miraculous TB healing, he was serving as art editor of a Christian youth publication, *The Covenant Companion*. The staff planned a Christian Life issue for February, 1924. Sallman took the assignment himself to draw something that would be a real challenge to their youth readers. Warner meditated on the theme for a long time and the day before the deadline he worked late at his drawing board, but to no avail. Sallman went to bed at midnight, restless in spirit but prayed once more for God to give him inspiration. He attempted to sleep. Suddenly at about 2:00 a clear, beautiful image of the head of Christ came into his mind. His studio was in his home, so he went immediately to his studio and worked as fast as he could to make a thumb-nail sketch while the details were still fresh in his mind. The next morning he made a charcoal drawing from his sketch and met the deadline for the magazine assignment. Years later he did an oil painting of the vision the Lord gave him and his paintings of Christ have become famous. He said, "I always think of the portrayal as something God did – through me. Ruth and I believe that as disciples of Christ, our task is primarily seed-sowing of good deeds, good thoughts and good purposes."

Curtis Hooper is a British artist whose portrait of Christ was published in *Life* magazine in 1984. Hooper spent seven years researching the Shroud of Turin, the cloth many feel actually wrapped the body of Christ at His burial. Curtis spent those seven years analyzing the image of Christ which appeared on the Shroud of Turin as well as analyzing all the photographs which have been taken of the image of Christ on the Shroud. He also consulted with all the specialists he could find to know how Jesus looked. After his seven years of research, Hooper painted his portrait of Christ which was published in *Life* magazine.

Hooper had a unique visitation of the Lord after he finished the portrait. He said that one day as he looked at the eyes of the Lord he had painted, the face of Jesus suddenly became real to him. The presence of the Lord overwhelmed him to the degree that it took him a year before he could really look at what he had painted. The Lord had stepped into the picture Hooper had painted and visited the artist.

Artist Nanette Crist was beginning a commissioned portrait of a client when the image of Jesus suddenly appeared beside her canvas. It was Easter time so she got another canvas and started painting a portrait of Jesus. The vision remained with her for three days while the painting was completed. Jesus told the artist He wanted His likeness painted so that it could be available to everyone.

Have there been photographs of the Lord? We know of several so we are sure there are many more that we have no record of. For example, on the afternoon of July 15, 1920, the young daughter of Mrs. Swanson, Seattle, Washington, asked her mother to take a picture of her surrounded by her playmates. Mrs. Swanson took her daughter's Brownie box camera and stood in a shadowed place and pointed the camera toward a bank of flowers while she waited for the children to gather for the picture. While she was waiting, Mrs. Swanson heard the camera click. Thinking the camera malfunctioned, she knew the film had been exposed so she rolled to the next frame. Again the camera spontaneously clicked, so again she rolled to the next frame. She held the shutter to prevent any more film being wasted. She used the last four frames to photograph her daughter and her playmates. When the film was developed, she found she had photographed the Lord standing in front of the flowers in her garden in the two frames that spontaneously clicked.

Also in the state of Washington, a Dr. Neeley from Roswell, New Mexico, was visiting and was asked to see a woman patient. After the house call, he went outside to take a picture of the patient's daughter. The camera snapped on its own and when the picture was developed there was a photo of the Lord.

In the fall of 1938, an elderly Christian woman of Oslo, Norway, felt she had back-slid in her relationship with the Lord. She prayed

daily for a sign that she was still His child. One day, the Holy Spirit spoke plainly saying, "Take your camera and go out into the garden and take a picture." Her prayer had been answered but she was so surprised that she tried to dismiss the instruction from her mind. But the Lord speaks twice, so the voice again repeated the instruction. She took her camera and randomly snapped a picture in her garden. When the film was developed, at first she didn't see anything of interest, but on a second look, the figure of Jesus burst into view. Her picture has been reproduced as a tract by both the Osterhus Publishing House and the Colportage Press of Minneapolis, MN.

In 1971 a Christian lady from California was traveling by car near Vincinnes, Indiana. She noted that the clouds were especially beautiful, so she took a picture. When the film was developed the Lord is seen floating in the clouds and in addition a number of angels with their wings visible were seen also surrounding Him.

During the Korean War a US reconnaissance plane took a picture of the ground below. There was scattered snow on the ground and when the film was developed the Lord's face appeared in the contrast of the snow and the bare ground.

In 1983 the *That's Incredible* TV program featured the story of a man who was driving his car and was suddenly guided to turn and drive a different route. On the new route he saw a building burning. As he was an amateur photographer, he took a picture of the burning building. When he developed the film he found there was a picture of the Lord instead of the burning building. As a result of the experience, he was healed of a sickness he had.

In a similar event, a traveler flying 20,000 feet over Texas in 1986 took a picture from the airplane window of the fog surrounding the plane. When the film was developed the Lord is seen in the fog. What thing is hard for the Lord? These experiences help us have faith that the Lord is always near.

DREAM VISITATIONS

*J*esus promises in the book of Revelation: "Behold, I stand at the door and knock; if any man hear my voice and open the door, I will come in to him and sup with Him and he with me" (3:20). God started His plan of visitation by walking with Adam and Eve in the cool of every morning (Gen 3:8). We are aware that the Bible is the record of God visiting his children whether his children are awake or asleep. Yes, the Lord can visit us while we are asleep during a dream. Let's first look at just a few of the visitations of God during our dreams as recorded in the written Word of God.

We know David was visited by the Lord in dreams for he said, "Thou has proved mine heart; thou hast visited me in the night" (17:3). Later David notes the importance of a dream visitation saying, "As for me, I will behold thy face in righteousness; I shall be satisfied, when I awake with thy likeness" (17:15).

Solomon, the son of David, was visited by the Lord in a dream. "In Gibeon the Lord appeared to Solomon in a dream by night; and God said, Ask what I shall give thee." Solomon replied, "Give therefore thy servant an understanding heart to judge thy people, that I may discern between good and bad: for who is able to judge this thy so great a people? And the speech pleased the Lord, that Solomon had asked this thing" (1st Kings 3: 5, 9).

A familiar visitation that occurred during sleep is the dream visitation of Jacob in Genesis, chapter 28. Jacob was traveling from Beersheba toward Haran and he tarried at a certain place because the sun was set and as he slept he dreamed of seeing a ladder that reached from earth to heaven with angels of God ascending and descending between heaven and earth. Jacob saw the Lord standing above the ladder and heard the blessing, which God pronounced, "Behold, I am with thee and will keep thee in all places whither thou goest...I will not leave thee until I have done that which I have spoken to thee of."

The visitation of the Lord always brings a blessing to us, just as it brought blessings to Jacob. Jacob said of His visitation: "This is none other but the house of God, and this is the gate of heaven" (Gen 28:17). We remember the story of how Joseph was able to interpret the dream of Pharaoh which led to his advancement in Pharaoh's kingdom. Joseph explained that Pharaoh's dream was doubled because "it is the thing is established by God, and God will shortly bring it to pass" (Gen 41:32). God speaks twice. Gideon used the spiritual law that God speaks twice to confirm that the message he received really was from God. First Gideon asked that the dew be on the fleece of wool, but that the floor be dry. Second, Gideon asked for the reverse; for dew to be on the floor but for the fleece to be dry (Judges 6:36-40).

The 33rd chapter of Job tells us more about how God speaks to us: "God speaketh once, yea twice, yet man perceiveth it not. In a dream, in a vision of the night, when deep sleep falleth upon men, in slumberings upon the bed; then He openeth the ears of men, and sealeth their instruction, that He may withdraw man from his purpose, and hide pride from man." When faced with a problem, we are familiar with the suggestion to "sleep on it." This allows the Lord to speak to us when our conscious mind is not in the way. We also need to be aware of the Lord's visitations to us during "slumberings"– that half awake and half asleep state when we are just dropping off to sleep or when we are in the process of waking up – alternating between being awake, then back asleep, and then awake again.

Joseph, Mary's husband, was instructed by dream for the safety of the baby Jesus. The book of Matthew tells us when Joseph found that Mary was with child, he was willing to put her away privily, but "the angel of the Lord appeared unto him in a dream, saying, Joseph, thou son of David, fear not to take unto thee Mary thy wife; for that which is conceived in her is of the Holy Ghost. And she shall bring forth a son, and thou shalt call his name JESUS: for He shall save His people from their sins" (Mt 1:20, 21). After the birth of Jesus the angel of the Lord again appeared to Joseph in a dream saying, "Arise, and take the young child and his mother, and flee into Egypt, and be thou there until I bring thee word: for Herod will seek the young child to destroy him" (Mat 2:13). Later, "But when Herod was dead, behold, an angel of the Lord appeared in a dream to Joseph in Egypt. Saying, Arise, and take the young child and his mother, and go into the land of Israel; for they are dead which sought the young child's life" (Mt 2:19, 20). Finally, by dream Joseph was warned not to return to Judea because Archelaus the son of Herod ruled Judea, so Joseph instead turned into the part of Galilee called Nazareth (Mt 2:22, 23).

We could review more examples of visitations of God and angels to men and women by dream as recorded in the Bible. Peter tells us: "be established in the present truth"(2nd Peter 1:12). Let us see how God uses dreams to visit us in our present day. We will relate several modern day dream visitations to strengthen your faith that the Lord can visit you - asleep or awake. His visitation brings the presence of God and the power of God which can change your life – for the better. Jesus continues God's plan to visit his creation for He promised, "Lo, I am with you always, even unto the end of the world" (Mt: 28:20).

The November 1984 issue of *The Saturday Evening Post* relates the dream visitation of Terry Cummings that changed his life. Terry was a basketball star first at DePaul University and later in the NBA When Terry was sixteen he admits he was unhappy and directionless during the summer he spent in Hammond, IN, with his grandmother. Here is Terry's account of his dream visitation:

"It was like the roof of the house disappeared and I could see straight up through the sky. And in the sky, I saw the clouds roll back and split open, and there was a fella on a white horse. He was dressed in white and wore a crown and there were a lot of other people behind him on white horses. I saw myself come out of the house and fall on my knees and start crying and screaming, "Lord, not now; I'm not ready!" But it was like the words I screamed had no power and the Lord didn't hear them. The fella on the first horse would speak, though, and his words would float through the air and tear up everything that was in disarray. And when I woke up the next morning, my bed was wet with sweat and I was still sweating and I had tears running down my face. My room was dark and I thought I'd lost all hope; that I was already in hell. But I looked at the curtains and saw a gleam of light and I realized that wherever there's a glitter of light there's hope. That day, I ran to the church and made up my mind that for whatever it was worth, from that point on it was gonna be me and Him all the way."

The dream visitation changed the life of Terry Cummings just as it changed the life of Jacob. A listener of the *Christ at the Door Ministry* broadcasts, John Wallace, told us his visitation, which occurred in a dream in the 1960s. In the dream John found himself on a street and in a line of people who were waiting to enter a building. A woman who was in the line of people asked John to come with her and go directly into the building. When they entered, they joined 75 to 100 other people. At the far end of the building, they saw a speaker talking to a few people. When all those assembled went over to hear the speaker, John was told to go through a side set of doors. As he followed the instruction he found that the side door of the building led directly into a large auditorium and he was in the back of this huge auditorium. John saw a long aisle leading down to the front and then a long flight of steps went upward.

Suddenly a person in the audience said, "There He is!" John looked up to the top of the steps and saw a man in a long white robe with his arms folded across His chest. Jesus had a beard and there was a crown on His head. John recognized the Lord and exclaimed, Jesus!" A counselor called John over to a booth, one of a series to the side of the auditorium. In each booth a counselor was instructing people. John's counselor explained that Jesus is coming to earth, but not just yet. The counselor told John what his work for the Lord was to be. John had seen the Lord; he had been instructed what his work for the Lord was. His visitation was complete and he soon woke up. His visitation was his call and he has followed that call.

Leland Wood received his call to serve the Lord by a dream. In the dream, Leland heard a knock at the door of his home. He saw part of his self staying in bed asleep while another part of his self went downstairs and answered the knock by opening the door. Leland recognized that the man knocking at the door was the Lord. The Lord appeared as a Hispanic spiritual man who greeted Leland by saying "Saluto, Amigo." The dream experience was Leland's hearing the knock of the Lord, answering the knock, opening the door and inviting the Lord into his life and home.

Linda Wood was a senior in high school when she had her dream visitation. In the dream she and her family were in their living room having their evening family devotions. Outside the living room, her attention in the dream was drawn to their dining room table. The family had a place setting for the Lord at the head of the table with a bible on His plate opened to Rev: 3:20 to symbolize that Jesus was invited to be the head of their family and they wished him to be present and sup with them at each meal. In the dream she saw a light begin to shine and increase in brilliance at the Lord's place at the head of the table. As the light increased in brilliance and substance the Lord's body began to take form in the light. As the Lord began to manifest, Linda felt her heart swell with love. Her heart started beating faster as she recognized she was in the presence of the Lord. The vision of the Lord in her dream was so vivid that she woke up. When she woke, she felt the fast beating of her heart. She had been sleeping on her stomach, so as she awoke, she turned over, opened her eyes, and behold, there was the Lord manifesting at the foot of her bed. The Lord at the foot of her bed looked the same as the vision that appeared at His place at the head of the dining room table while she was asleep. In the joy of seeing the Lord while awake, she noticed that her bed was actually shaking with each heartbeat, her joy was so great. She praised the Lord as He remained in view. Soon the presence of the Lord and His brilliance slowly decreased and Linda continued praising God as her heart returned to normal.

In 2013 Dr. Reggie Anderson (with Jennifer Schuchmann) wrote *Appointments with Heaven: The True Story of a Country Doctor's Healing Encounters with the Hereafter* (2013, Tyndale Momentum). Dr. Anderson had two significant modern day visitations during dreams. The first dream: In June, 1962, Dr. Anderson was a four and a half-year-old boy living in Plantersville, Alabama. He enjoyed watching The Popeye Show on their black and white TV. Reggie responded to a TV contest to win a Shetland pony by sending a post-card with his name for the drawing. In his dream Reggie was riding the contest pony bareback in a red clover field. A voice with authority spoke to Reggie saying, "You will win this pony, but you must share this gift with everyone who wants to ride this special horse. To whom much is given, much is expected." Reggie recognized that the voice in the dream was God speaking to him. The visitation of God came to pass. Reggie won the pony.

In his book Dr. Anderson tells his complete boyhood story of growing up and losing his faith in God when his cousins were brutally murdered in the 1973 Alday brothers massacre in Donalsonville, Georgia. Why didn't God prevent the massacre? Why? Because God didn't exist, Reggie falsely reasoned. His secular faith in science grew as he graduated from college and entered medical school at the University of Alabama in Birmingham. But his secular faith was beginning to crack. He met a Christian girl and he began to attend catechism classes with a Catholic priest.

The Gospel of Visitation

A visitation of the Lord during a dream put Dr. Anderson's life back on track. Over a 4th of July week-end break from medical school classes, Reggie took a solitary camping trip to a wilderness area. That evening he read *Mere Christianity* by C.S. Lewis plus the gospel of John, finishing by the light of his flashlight. Falling into a deep sleep he had a second visitation experience. In his dream he was in heaven and enjoying the serenity, beauty and peace of heaven. Soon he saw a crowd of people moving toward him and he recognized them as the Alday cousins who had been murdered. They communicated to him that they were there to lift the burden he had been carrying. They communicated that he should not hold their misfortune against God. And he understood. His burden was lifted.

Next he saw a man emerge and he recognized this man as Jesus. Jesus said to him, "Reggie, why are you running from me? Your friends are here with me in paradise; you can stop running." With Jesus' words Reggie could also feel the warmth and love from the presence of Jesus wrap around his heart and soul. Jesus said, "I am the one who came for you." Reggie realized he was being rescued from his seven years of hate, anger and aimless wandering in his spiritual wilderness. Jesus said, "Your friends and family are here, and they have been made whole." Reggie could see how his Alday cousins no longer had the scars of their murder; they were now whole and perfect. Jesus said, "I have a plan for you, but you need to stop running." Jesus told Reggie His plan for his life, who he would marry, how many children he would have and where he would practice as an M.D. Jesus final words were, "All I have told you will come to pass. All you have to do is trust in me and in my words."

Reggie awoke from his incredible journey and realized he did not deserve a visitation of the Lord. He felt the weight of his sins of unbelief and knew he needed to do something to cleanse himself of his past. So he hiked to a nearby pool and let the waterfall baptize him as he cried tears of remorse and tears of repentance. His dream visitation healed him of unbelief and gave him a new way to live daily in the presence of Jesus Christ his Lord. His book recounts how he is aware that the Lord guides him daily in his medical practice.

We are familiar with near death experiences in which a patient dies and visits heaven before being resuscitated and returned to life. Reggie's experience is unique in that he did not have to undergo a painful death to visit heaven, only a painful loss of his faith. Near death experiencers seem to have an increased spiritual awareness. The same is true in Dr. Anderson's life. In his medical practice Dr. Anderson has had the privilege of being with many patients at their death. He has noticed what he calls "the gaze of glory." That is, the patient looks up and to the right shortly before they die. Their gaze is relaxed and peaceful with an almost otherworldly quality. Many times he has sensed a slight breeze which is mixed with a warm sensation and he has felt this warmth pass by his cheek. Many times he can smell a fragrance of lilac and citrus. By being spiritually aware, he has had many glimpses of heaven in the daily lives of his patients; especially as he has sat beside patients going through the transition of earthly life to heavenly life.

Some people have been critical of near death experiences because what they experience seems too good to be true. Everyone seems to get to go to heaven. Dr. Anderson tells the death experience of a patient he calls Eddie. Eddie had the reputation for being a bad man with a horrible temper. Dr. Anderson had treated many of the victims of Eddie's anger when he drank too much. Eddie thrived on being mean and hurting others; he was truly evil. Eddie was dying of cancer and Dr. Anderson tried to witness to Eddie for a deathbed conversion, but Eddie refused. Dr. Anderson was present at his passing and Eddie seemed to be staring off into a great chasm. He eyes grew wide in fear and he was restless and anxious. Instead of being peaceful, Eddie struggled with each breath and his last breath was a grunt.

Dr. Anderson felt a type of dark cloud was present in the room; the temperature plummeted. He smelled sulfur and diesel; Dr. Anderson felt that evil had entered the room and noted that everything about Eddie's death was the antithesis of the heavenly experiences he usually felt when his other patients died. Dr. Anderson notes: "I believe that when Eddie crossed over to the other side, he didn't like what he found." Dr. Anderson wanted to get out of the room as fast as he could; so he did. Praise the Lord for His plan of visitation. Jesus Christ can also visit you for His promise is: "My sheep hear my voice, and I know them, and they follow me: And I give unto them eternal life…" (John 10:27, 28)

In 1934 Starr Daily wrote *Love Can Open Prison Doors* (Willing Publishing Co.). As a boy, Starr had recurring dreams of Jesus. In the dream, the young boy of about 12 would be in a strange beautiful garden. The garden was in a shoe-shaped valley surrounded by gently sloping hills. At the end of the valley a white-gray rock jutted out, and from behind it Jesus would emerge and walk toward Starr. Despite his dreams of Jesus, Starr began a series of minor crimes in his youth and before he had grown out of his teens, he had already been in prison twice. He became known as one of the greatest safecrackers alive. He was part of a gang that robbed bank after bank. Finally he was arrested and sent to prison again. He hated God and in his criminal mind set he hated everything, including himself. His hate caused attacks of indigestion and constipation. He was a terror in prison and constantly fought others. When it was discovered that he was planning to incite a prison riot, he was sent to the hole, an eight by eight foot cell. He was in solitary confinement until he would apologize to the warden for his actions. But in his criminal mindset he decided he would die rather than apologize to the warden. But his strength was ebbing away because the warden also had Starr on a bread and water diet. As his blood sugar plummeted on this diet, Starr had a dream.

In his dream Starr was again in the same garden where Jesus had visited him when he was 12. Again Jesus walked toward Starr. Jesus looked down at Starr in love. Starr felt the love of Jesus and had never felt so utterly enveloped in love. His soul seemed to know that he was seeing something and feeling something that would influence his life from now to all eternity. Jesus seemed to slowly fade from view and next there emerged a vision of the word "*Love*" Soon the word "*Love*" also vanished. Starr woke up from the dream, but the quality of the dream seemed to linger and become a part of him. After receiving the Lord's love, Starr felt himself exuding love. Instead of the hate he formerly had, now he seemed to escape all the limitations that had formerly tortured him. His whole being seemed to be a manifestation of this universal love he had experienced when Jesus visited him. His bitterness and stubbornness was gone.

He was suddenly able to use his mind in a new and unusual way. As a mental exercise, he would invite imaginary special guests to his prison cell to discuss subjects of life and truth. During these imaginary symposiums he held in his mind he received more about the creative power of love. So he began applying the power of love because the Love of God remained in him. He realized God's love not only was transforming him but came to him through no conscious efforts of his own. Jesus visited and left His love, which transformed Starr Daily into a new creature. Instead of maintaining his tiff with the warden he was able to think of the warden with an all-consuming passion. Soon he was unexplainably released from solitary confinement. He began to apply love in his life by starting to do constructive deeds for his fellow prisoners and he soon found that he no longer had any enemies in prison. His change was so dramatic that he was soon released early from his sentence, hence the title of his book: *Love Can Open Prison Doors*.

Starr wrote that love is God in action. And in the process of accepting the doctrine of love, one grows into oneness with God. A visitation by dream turned Starr's life around and changed his former criminal mind into a new creature in Christ able to love instead of hate. After his first book he wrote many more books about the Christian life.

G. Scott Sparrow, author of *I am with you Always, True Stories of Encounters with Jesus* (Bantam, 1995), like Starr Daily had his first visitation of the Lord by a dream in 1975. His own dream visitations are also noted in his 1976 *Lucid Dreaming—Dawning of the Clear Light*. Lucid dreaming is the experience of becoming aware that one is dreaming during the dream. Job reminds us that Jesus visitations can occur asleep as well as awake.

Near Death Visitation

The written Word of God tells us to "be established in the present truth" (2nd Peter 1:12). That is, be aware of what the Living Word of God, Jesus Christ, is revealing to us in our present day. Paul exhorted the Hebrews to "See that ye refuse not him that speaketh" (12:25). Jesus told Pilate, "Every one that is of the truth heareth my voice" (Jn. 18:37). Jesus promises in the book of Revelation that He is right at our door and ready to speak to us (Rev.3:20).

Because of medical advances in the ability to resuscitate dying patients, patients who a few decades ago would have died, have now been brought back to life and back from their journey to heaven. Dr. Sam Parnia, M.D., Ph.D. in *Erasing Death: The Science That is Rewriting the Boundaries Between Life and Death*, (2013, Harper Collins) explains in detail the recent medical advances that have enabled doctors to be successful in bring back to life patients that have died. After their return, these patients have retained some memory of what happened to them in heaven. These experiences have happened to so many people that their stories are now called Near Death Experiences. The Near Death Experience (NDE) literature has kept us abreast of the ever increasing number of near death experiences. The Bible carries the promise that Jesus comes to earth to visit us in our abode. ("If any man hear My voice, and open the door, I will come in to him, and will sup with him, and he with Me.") The NDE is the ultimate visitation experience because those who have died and returned tell us of their visit to Jesus at His abode. Some who have returned from death have briefly seen friends and relatives. Others who have died and gone to heaven have had a private visitation with the Lord. One of the first Americans to experience a NDE and write about it was George Ritchie.

In 1943 George Ritchie was 20 and enlisted in the army. In September while at Camp Barkeley in Abilene, TX, he died and had a near death experience. After his NDE, he attended medical school and become an M.D. In 1952 he started speaking in public about his NDE. In 1963 he wrote an article in *Guidepost* magazine about his NDE which he expanded into a book in 1978 titled *Return from Tomorrow*. In 1965 Raymond Moody, 20, was an undergraduate student at the University of Virginia and heard of Ritchie's NDE. This sparked an interest for Moody and ten years later in 1975 Moody published *Life After Life*, his first book about NDEs.

A psychology professor at the University of Connecticut, Dr Kenneth Ring, read Moody's book. As a psychologist, Ring had an interest in out-of-body reports, mystical experiences at death and other altered states of consciousness, so Moody's *Life After Life* caught Professor Ring's attention. Reading Moody's book lifted the professor out of a personal problem of serious depression. Before reading *Life After Life* Dr. Ring said he felt spiritually adrift as if he had somehow lost his way. He tried volunteer work; he tried studying philosophy; but these activities didn't help lift his depression. Reading the near death experiences of others seemed to be an answer for Ring. He said these experiences, "combined with a certain quality of luminous serenity which many near-death survivors display, made me feel that I myself was undergoing an extended spiritual awakening. " Ring joined Moody in interviewing NDErs and these interviews continued to help Ring have a spiritual awakening. Like Professor Ring, it is our prayer that you, the reader, can also have a spiritual awakening as you read the NDE visitation experiences of others. Moody's book was so popular that in 1977 he published a second book *Reflections on Life*

After Life. Ring also followed with a sequel *Heading Toward Omega* in 1984.

In 1978, Moody, Ring and other researchers formed the Association for the Scientific Study of Near Death Phenomena. Later the name was changed to the International Association of Near Death Studies. In 1982 a Gallup poll estimated that eight million Americans have had a NDE. When Gallup re-polled in 1992 the estimate was increased to thirteen million. Gallup published *Adventures in Immortality* which is based on his surveys.

In addition to no longer fearing the event of death, survivors of these near death experiences as a result of their visitation experience and the love they experienced in heaven, return to life with a renewed commitment to the Lord. Many returned with the message that Jesus told them to tell His people that he is returning soon. Most have a renewed interest in the Bible. They no longer have a fear of death

As authors relate their heavenly experiences, we can learn with them the value of present day truth. For example, what about suicide? Angie Fenimore in her 1995 book *Beyond the Darkness: My Near-Death Journey to the Edge of Hell and Back* warns others who may be contemplating suicide. Angie briefly died from her suicide attempt and when she met God, God said :

"Is this what you really want? Don't you know that this is the worst thing you could have done?" She replied, "But my life is so hard." His response: "You think that was hard? It is nothing compared to what awaits you if you take your life" (p 191).

Soon Angie was aware of another being who had complete and perfect empathy for her. She realized she was in the presence of the Redeemer of the world.

He said, "Don't you understand? I have done this for you."

The Gospel of Visitation

Angie's spiritual eyes were opened and she was able to see things from His point of view. She suddenly knew how and when she had gone wrong. She had doubted His existence and she had questioned the authenticity of the Scriptures because what they claimed seemed too good to be true. She realized that suicide was the most selfish act she could ever have been capable of. It was an act of vanity. In the love which the Lord brought she understood:

"I now saw that I was never forced to come to this earth. I could see that before my birth, I knew what I would face, and that with God, I had co-authored the course of my life; I knew that confusion and heartache would be my companions. I chose my parents and even several of my friends before I came to earth. The option to have an easier life was always mine, but I volunteered, I sacrificed...I knew what to expect, and still I chose to come. We all make that choice" (p 137).

In his 2013 book *Revealing Heaven: The Case for Near-Death Experiences*, Episcopal priest John W. Price tells the effect on his life and ministry of hearing more than two hundred NDEs. Unfortunately he also tells of his experience of telling Episcopal seminary professors in Austin about NDEs only to have his witness of the truth rejected. Price ends his book by saying (p 158):

"From the annals of the near-death experiences, we know God loves, forgives, and redeems all people when they ask. As well, God lovingly brings us on into heaven for the continuing journey of our lives. The accounts of the near-death experiences need to be shouted from the rooftops, as they tell us such profound truths."

As just one example of the profound truths NDEs bring to us, Eben Alexander, M.D. in *Proof of Heaven: A Neurosurgeon's Journey*

Into the Afterlife (Simon & Schuster Paperbacks, 2012) brings us present day truths: "At the risk of oversimplifying, I was allowed to die harder, and travel deeper, than almost all NDE subjects before me" (p 78). Alexander explains that "If we knew too much of the spiritual realm now, then navigating our lives on earth would be an even greater challenge than it already is" (p 81). Eben was given a tour, accompanied by his guardian angel, a kind of grand overview of the invisible, spiritual side of existence. But they could not go into the higher regions of heaven for this reason. The overall message he received was that he was loved. He said (p 73):

> "The unconditional love and acceptance that I experienced on my journey is the single most important discovery I have ever made, or will ever make, and as hard as I know it's going to be to unpack the other lessons I learned while there, I also know in my heart that sharing this very basic message—one so simple that most children readily accept it—is the most important task I have."

He says we get closer to our genuine spiritual self by manifesting love and compassion.

We can learn something about God from each NDE. We listen to Matthew, Mark, Luke, and John because they walked with the Lord. And we can be established in present day truth because those who had a NDE also walked with the Lord while they were briefly in heaven. For example listen to the witness of Dr. Gary Wood (p 62, *A Place Called Heaven*, 2008 Tate Publishing & Enterprises, LLC):

> "Then Jesus looked right at me with those piercing blue eyes and said, 'Don't ever buy the condemnation of the devil that you are unworthy. You are worthy. You have been redeemed by the Blood of the Lamb." Jesus said, "Why do my people not believe in me? Why do my people reject me? Why do they not walk in my commandments?"

Dr. Gary Wood said Jesus commissioned him to make Him real to the people of this earth. He said that there would be three things that would mark His soon return: A Spirit of Restoration, A Spirit of Prayer, and an Outburst of Miracles. Jesus told me, "Remember what I say, for the Father and I are one. When I speak, the Father has spoken. Above all else love one another and always be forgiving towards each other." Jesus showed Gary that our planet earth is encircled by three rings:

> "Inside the first ring, the earth's atmosphere, I saw hundreds of evil spirits. This is Satan's domain. The evil spirits would target people and try to deceive them. If the people would accept the lies as truth, many more demons would swarm in like flies. They would then begin to fall to the temptations of the flesh by allowing the demons to control them, and their lives would begin to fall apart. The demons have power to make people tell lies, cheat, steal, commit adultery, and speak evil against one another. It was like the people became puppets on a string. Then Jesus showed me that when a child of God got down on their knees before Him, praying in the name of Jesus, with faith, their prayers would shoot into the heavens like barbed arrows. An army of angelic forces would appear, prepared for battle to destroy the demons' effectiveness. The more prayers of faith there were, the more the demons would retreat. But if doubt and unbelief were spoken, the demons would begin to overcome. The Lord told me that as time grows closer to His return, demon activity will become more rampant. Satan knows that the final curtain is being drawn, and his time is running out" (pp 71-72).

We need to remember that Gary suffered the pain of an auto accident at age eighteen to bring back and share with us these words of Jesus for our day. We are familiar with the Old Testament and the

New Testament. When Peter tells us to be established in the present truth, this reminds us that those who have been privileged to return from dying are bringing us a present day new testament to prepare us for His Second Return. As a result of what Gary learned in heaven he says, "I have come to believe that, beyond a shadow of a doubt, the greatest need of mankind is prayer" (p 73).

All NDExperiencers return with the knowledge that their heavenly experience was a love feast. For example Dean Braxton *In Heaven! Experiencing the Throne of God* (2009. Xulon Press) writes:

> "He is sending love to each and every person on the planet. All the time love from God is being sent out to each and every person and nothing can stop this love from reaching us. We can deny His love, reject His love or act like His love is not there, but He keeps sending it to us...I have stated this before, that every time we take a breath of air, he is saying, 'I love you.'"

Some Christians have rejected NDEs because they sound too good to be true. Barbara R. Rommer is an M.D. who after interviewing three hundred NDEs wrote *Blessings in Disguise: Another Side of the Near Death Experience* (2000, Llewellyn). She speaks of LTPs (Less Than Positive) NDEs. She found that 17.7 percent had these less than positive NDEs and she feels the LTP can be the impetus to self-introspection, which will ultimately cause positive changes. She tells the story of Sadira who went to hell after an overdose. She survived and returned to life feeling absolutely terrified yet with a renewed hope. She said, "Suicide can never be the answer. This is not an option. God does not want this. I believe in God very strongly. He will not excuse this. I saw hell!"

Peter tells us to be established in present day truth. The people who have suffered the pain of dying before visiting heaven and returning to life can bring us present day truth. The subject of homosexuality divides

Christendom. True, the scriptures tell us that Paul admonished against homosexuals. Because of this some Christians feel homosexuals can't go to heaven. (The scriptures also approve of slavery, but now we realize we are living in a different age.) What is God's attitude? Liz Dale, Ph.D., R.N. in *Crossing Over and Coming Home: 21 Authors Discuss the Gay Near-Death Experience as Spiritual Transformation* (2001, Llewellyn) gives us present day truth. Andre, one of the 21 gay authors of Dale's book, died in 1991 when his appendix burst. Andre first heard a voice declare over and over, "I stand at the door and knock." When Andre became accustomed to his heavenly surroundings he asked the spiritual beings, "Is it o.k. to be gay?" The spiritual beings laughed and said, "Who do you think made gay people?" Andre remembered that he laughed with his spiritual guides for what seemed like a thousand years over the absurdity of his question. He said he felt like he fit in for the first time in his entire life; completely fit in as a gay man in God's heaven. He remembers that heaven was so beautiful that it was as if on earth all the colors are in black and white, but in heaven the colors were alive and vibrated.

We need to remember that each NDExperiencer first suffered the pain of their death. We can be grateful that they are willing to share their experiences which gives us present day truth about their visitation to heaven. New books are written each year about NDE which helps open the veil between earth and heaven for the reader. Their visitation experiences can help us seek the kingdom of God and His right-use-ness. The Lord can speak to us as we read the accounts of what the Lord told each author as they visited Jesus in His abode.

TRANCE VISITATIONS AND OTHER NON-NEAR DEATH VISITATIONS

Rev 3:20 promises that Jesus Christ is right at our door to visit us. Our privilege is to open our door and welcome the Lord to guide our life. The Lord comes from His home in heaven to briefly visit us at our home on earth. Many Christians in a NDE have had the blessing of briefly visiting Him in His heavenly home. When we read the experience of a person who has died and gone to heaven before being resuscitated and returned to life, we are privileged to gain insights about our future home in heaven. Christians pray to have the blessing when we die of going to heaven so we can walk with the Lord daily and continuously.

There are visits to heaven some Christians have been privileged to have that didn't require them to nearly die. Some have fallen into a trance and a heavenly messenger has taken them to visit heaven. *Nine Days in Heaven: A True Story* (2011, Charisma House) is the story of the trance visitation of Marietta Davis in 1848. Authors Dennis and Nolene Prince edited and brought the archaic language up to date of the original book *Scenes Beyond the Grave* originally written by John Laughran Scott. They also added footnotes to each chapter to correlate Marietta's experiences to Bible passages.

During a revival during the winter of 1847-48, Marietta's mother and two sisters found the reality of their faith but Marietta did not. But in August of 1848 Marietta fell into a trance and the Angel of

Peace accompanied her to heaven. For nine days she was shown the life humans are privileged to live in heaven. Before she was returned to her body on earth the Lord spoke: "Child, it is important that you return. You have a commission. Be faithful to it. Whenever you have an opportunity, tell people what you have seen and heard. Fulfill your mission, and, at the appointed time, angels will meet you at the gate of death and carry you to your home here in the kingdom of peace" (p 190). Marietta fulfilled her mission for seven months and then she was privileged to return to heaven and enter into the joy of her lord.

Another example of a trance visitation to heaven was announced by a full page ad in the April 1985 issue of *The Saturday Evening Post*. In this ad Dr. Collett, a medical missionary, stated: "I walked in Heaven with Jesus." The ad offered for sale 12 audio tapes describing Dr. Collett's five and a half day stay in Heaven. A year later in 1986 Dr. Collett with a co-author wrote the book *I Walked in Heaven with Jesus*.

Dr. Collett was born in England and was raised by Christian parents. When he was a small boy, he was privileged to have an angel visitation. He was 12 years old when the First World War started and 17 years old when it ended. He came to the United States in 1920 to study to be a missionary and in 1925 at the age of 23 he made his first missionary journey up the Amazon River. After years of preaching, evangelism, and missionary work Dr. Collett began asking in prayer, "Oh, God, let me see thy glory." As he prayed he would often dream about being in heaven. Dr. Collett prayed "Oh, God, let me see thy glory" for seven years. After seven years Dr. Collett was worshiping God in the Amazon region of South American with the native church congregation he helped establish. The congregation was of one accord and united in prayer when Dr. Collett entered a trance and his soul left his body.

The same angel that had visited Dr. Collett as a small boy said to him, "We are going to take the journey." In his soul body, Dr. Collett noted that his angel was to his left side. As they looked into the sky they saw the angel of the Lord coming to them. The angel of the Lord settled to the right of Dr. Collett. In the angel of the Lord's right hand was a flaming sword of fire. The angel of the Lord said, "I have come from God the Father to take you to heaven. We are leaving right now." Many NDExperiencers enter a tunnel which rapidly takes them to heaven. But because Dr. Collett had not died, but was instead in a trance, while his physical body remained in the Amazon, their travel to heaven which was three trillion miles away, took six hours. Dr. Collett spent five and a half days in heaven and returned with permission to write about some of his experiences. Dr. Collett found that the planet we call heaven has seven levels with one level at the outer perimeter just outside heaven's gates where those souls are located who have work to complete before they can fully enter heaven. He reported that inside the second gate is the third heaven which Paul speaks about in 2nd Corinthians 12:2. God with Jesus on his right hand is the top throne in the seventh heaven. The city four square of Rev. 21:16 Dr. Collett found to be 1,500 miles in height. The Throne of God Dr. Collett found has a base of over 2,000 miles and is 2,000 miles high.

Dr. Collett writes (p 72), "Jesus still sits at the right hand of God, the Father and yet Jesus can appear anywhere, any place or many places at one time. This is the wonderful, glorious reality of Jesus; because he is our Savior and He can come to us anywhere, anytime." Dr. Collett explains that (p 28) "what the Lord has shown to me, is not a new doctrine or revelation; it is a fuller revelation of the Spirit, not adding any words to the Bible, or any new thing, or new organization, or a new word, but a revelation of the true Word of God." After he woke from his trance, he continued his missionary work in the Amazon. When he finished his missionary work among the Amazon Indians he returned to the US. In addition to writing his book and recording his tapes, he continued his ministry in Florida.

Kit Kerr in her book and tapes *Revealing Heaven I and II* (2007, 2011, Xulon Press) has the unique blessing to be caught up by the

Spirit of God without having to die. The Lord visited her in her home many times before He commissioned her to write about His home. She was taken by the Spirit of God on tours of heaven for over ten years before she wrote her first book. The foreword of the first book was written by two scribe angels who were assigned to assist her in writing the rest of her books. As a result of her unique spiritual gift she has been commissioned to reveal details of heaven and give hope to all Christians for Eternity. Details such as "the portal" where heaven's citizens are allowed to see many things concerning their families on earth (p 110, Vol. II). The "creation lab" where heaven's citizens can stand on a platform and in hologram form watch how God created the original earth (p 50, vol II). The "Hall of Knowledge" where information is kept on almost any subject in towers of books that you watch as a hologram instead of reading (p 56, Vol. II). "Word University" where heaven's citizens are taught the revealed word of God instead of just head knowledge (p 46, Vol. II). "Royal University" where heavenly citizens receive education and training to rule and reign with Christ in the new earth (p 49, Vol II). "Hall of Super Heroes" filled with the faces of intercessors who now live in heaven. She watched a spiritual sword form from their prayers and the angel of the Lord grab the weapon their words had just created and depart to fight the enemy concerning what they had just prayed (p 126, Vol. II).

The most thrilling parts of her book is her descriptions of the throne of God located in the third heaven and the worship of heavenly citizens before the throne. Kit explains that salvation is free but the way we live our life now determines our eternal position. Kit gives practical advice: each morning as we awake we can look up to heaven and pray, "Father, I ask for and receive Grace for this day, Amen." This allows us to download from heaven, heavenly fuel for each day as we prepare for our heavenly citizenship through His Grace.

Kenneth Ring, a University of Connecticut psychology professor, wrote about NDEs in *Heading Toward Omega – In Search of the*

Meaning of the Near-Death Experience (1984, Wm. Morrow). His book, of course, tells the NDEs of many people. But he also tells a visitation experience of Nancy Clark who wrote to Ring to share her 1979 visitation experience. In January of 1979 Nancy had a dream that a close friend of hers had died. Indeed she later learned that within an hour of her dream, her friend had indeed died in a plane crash. Soon she was invited to give the eulogy at her close friend's funeral. As she began her eulogy, all of a sudden she became aware of a brilliant white light which was coming from the left rear of the chapel at ceiling level. She saw this light with an inner awareness, not with her human eyes. She recognized that this light was God because there was transference of knowledge that God placed directly into her consciousness. Next she felt God's light completely surrounding her. She felt as if she had merged completely with the light and belonged to it. She felt a greater sense of reality and truth in God's presence and felt as if she was home.

Nancy felt a love from God emanating from the light. God's love and presence of course was beyond her human words to describe. God's love gave her the feeling that she was in a state of grace. She felt all her sins were forgiven and she felt totally free in Christ. Next God spoke to her and gave her His blessing with His words. She didn't hear the words with her human ears but rather God's thoughts were placed directly in her consciousness. Her visitation lasted several minutes and occurred simultaneously while she was delivering her eulogy. She was completely in God's presence and at the same time she was completely aware of her surroundings and the eulogy she was delivering.

Immediately, Nancy said, God's visitation transformed her into a brand new person. She had a deeper love and unity with everyone and everything that she came in contact with. She had a greater awareness of all living things. She had awareness that we are all a part of one another and that we are ultimately a part of the greater consciousness of God. She knew God had elevated her to a higher level of spirituality. Before her visitation she had no formal religious training but after her visitation she joined a church and began reading the Bible to learn more about God. Best of all, her old negative image of herself was changed and she saw herself as worthy in God's eyes because He had visited her. Even though she didn't know why God chose to visit her, she was grateful and praised God for His grace. Nancy did not have to die and return; but perhaps because of her friend's sudden death and her eulogy at the funeral, God visited her.

Jeffrey Furst's *Edgar Cayce's Story of Jesus: Selections, Arrangements and Comments* (1969, Conward-McCann) is just one of over three hundred books about Cayce and his unique psychic ability to relax and enter into a trance-like sleep state. In studying the readings of Cayce, Furst states that "within the Readings, he continually warned against communication with 'the dead' – and all such occupations as automatic writing, séances, table tapping, Ouija boards, and the like" (p 302). Did Cayce have a visitation of the Lord? Cayce states that by age fourteen he had read the Bible through several times and "as I read its promises and the prayers of those who sought to commune with the One God, I felt that it must be true. I had a religious experience, a vision and a promise (a promise that to me is still very sacred)." In his private life, Cayce was a devout Christian as a result of his early life religious experience.

In his clairvoyant sleep-state Cayce answered questions asked by the seeker. However Furst notes that at times personages would come spontaneously and speak through Cayce as a medium. For example on August 6, 1933, a study group requested a reading be given on Jesus the Christ. The reading (5749-4) began "I John, would speak with thee concerning the Lord, the Master, as He walked among men. As given, if all that He did and said were written, I suppose the world would not contain all that may be said. As He, the Christ, is in His glory that was ordained of the Father, He may be approached by those who in sincerity and earnestness seek to know Him—and to be guided by Him..." After recording the full reading, Furst notes (p

302), "Certainly this was not Edgar Cayce speaking in the first person. Is this then a direct message from John of the Revelation or how shall we regard it?"

On another occasion Cayce had been quite ill and weak. He was giving a reading for himself asking for help for his own sickness. During the reading his voice was weak but suddenly after a pause a powerful and loud voice spoke in anger: "Bow thine heads, ye children of men! For I, Michael, Lord of the way, would speak with thee! Ye generation of vipers—ye adulterous generation—be warned! There is today set before thee good and evil! Choose thou whom ye will serve! Walk in the way of the Lord—or else there will come that sudden reckoning, as ye have seen! Bow thine heads, ye who are ungracious, unrepentant! For the glory of the Lord is at hand! The opportunity is before thee—accept or reject!" (294-100). Furst explains (p 307) that there had been some ambivalence in purpose concerning the work of Edgar Cayce.

Reading 993 was given in response to the question, "Might I receive at this time a message from the Master? The reading in part: "…In choosing me, as I have chosen you, there comes that beauty of oneness in knowing the way that brings to others peace, joy, happiness, in doing His will; for he that seeks to do His will may in me have that peace, that joy, that understanding, that gives to each in their respective spheres their needs, their desires, as their desires are in me. Be faithful…" Furst comments (p 313), "Is this not a direct message from the Master, or how then shall we regard it?"

On 12/16/36 members of the Association for Research and Enlightenment, Inc. sought a reading for counsel and guidance in carrying forward their work. Two parts of the 254-92 reading are significant: "Hence the ideals and the purposes of the Association for Research & Enlightenment, Inc., are not to function as another schism or ism. Keep away from that! For these warnings have been given again and again. Less and less of personality, more and more of God and Christ in the dealings with thy fellow man" (p 328). "In the bodily functioning, then, the activities are to have due and proper consideration, to be sure. But let each phase of the Work present how not only mentally but spiritually there is a grounding in TRUTH, as is set forth in the Christ-Consciousness as exemplified by Jesus, as has been proclaimed by many of the saints of old. And then ye may be very sure that all of those influences from the spiritual realm are as ONE. FOR WHETHER IT BE AS YE HAVE SEEN AT TIMES, THE LORD OF THE WAY OR THE CHRIST HIMSELF AS JESUS, OR OTHERS BE SENT AS AN AID, depends upon whether ye hold that ideal that is One with the Universal Truth for and to man" (p 329).

For another trance visitation let's look at *The Final Quest* by Rick Joyner (1995, Whitaker House). Rick was given a panoramic vision of the last battle between light and darkness. His prophetic experience was given over a period of one year and started with a dream. "Some of it came under a very intense sense of the presence of the Lord, but the overwhelming majority was received in some level of a trance" (p 11). "In the dream and the trances, I had what I consider to be greatly magnified gifts of discernment and words of knowledge" (p 12). Joyner explains there are four levels of prophetic revelation: first are impressions and visions; second, "a conscious sense of the presence of the Lord, or the anointing of the Holy Spirit which gives special illumination to our minds (p 10); third, open visions which are "external, and are viewed with the clarity of a movie screen" (p 10); fourth, trances which "are like dreaming when you are awake. Instead of just seeing a 'screen' like an open vision, you feel like you are in the movie, that you are actually there in a strange way" (p 11).

David E Taylor wrote *Face-to-Face Appearances from Jesus: The Ultimate Intimacy* in 2009. David is an evangelist who was commissioned at 18 to preach the gospel. David tells his journey to come into the presence of the Lord, face to face until in 2000 the Lord took David on a special trip to heaven which is told in his 2011 *My Trip to Heaven: Face to Face with Jesus*. David was privileged to meet Smith Wigglesworth who ministered in the early 1900s and God used to raise twenty-three people from the dead. Smith didn't read any book but the Bible while he ministered on earth, but told David to "go back and study the great men and women that God used in a significant way" (p 155). Kathryn Kuhlman told David, "Don't stop preaching the word of God, and furthermore, don't desecrate!" David saw the beautiful city of God: Mount Zion. When he was privileged to worship before God's throne, "Jehovah God was in front of me, but I couldn't see His face. He allowed me to draw close to Him as much as I could, but the power, light, and glory from His presence were too overwhelming so that I was only able to come to His feet. Jesus was standing next to me, and He helped me to endure the glory coming from His Father.... When I got as close as I could to the Father, I saw that He loves and longs to be worshipped and adored in a certain way. As I observed Him and His character, I realized that He wanted more than just praise. He longed to be reverenced, adored, worshipped, and honored. It was beyond praise! He desired true worship manifested in spirit and in truth."

We can learn more about God's plan of visitation as we review the unusual visits to heaven by those still alive. Jesus comes through our door to visit His modern day disciples in many different ways.

DISGUISE VISITATIONS

*I*n the 18th chapter of Genesis we remember the story of three strangers who visited Abraham. Were the strangers angels in disguise or were the strangers the Lord in disguise? In our day, the Lord can still visit in disguise. For example: In the 1940s a mother and daughter team both named Katherine Stubergs spent five years sculpting wax figures of da Vinci's famous Last Supper. The citizens of Santa Cruz, CA, purchased the wax figures in 1951 and the exhibit was presented at the Santa Cruz Art League Galleries at 526 Broadway without admission charge for the enjoyment and inspiration of the public until 1997. In the late 1950s Alice Stockett, a member of the Christ at the Door Ministry, and her husband had the opportunity to view the exhibit and sit in front of the wax figures of the disciples with other tourists. The wax figures were so lifelike that in the quiet of the room they felt they were a part of the Lord with his disciples at the Last Supper. After the tourist group sat in awe and silence, they gathered in the rear of the gallery behind their seats to compare their reactions to the life-size exhibit.

Alice was conversing with another man about the likeness of the Lord when she suddenly realized that this man in referring to the Lord used the pronoun "I" instead of "He." She realized she was talking to the Lord in disguise. He was wearing a business suit and appeared as a kindly older man. Just as soon as she reached this conclusion, the man excused himself from the conversation and mysteriously disappeared. She looked high and low and He was nowhere to be found in the group of tourists. Then she felt sure her impression was correct. The Lord had appeared in disguise and visited her in this way. Her heart rejoiced as she realized she had been in the actual presence of the Lord.

In downtown Los Angeles, Clifton's Cafeteria opened for business during the depression. It was known as the "Cafeteria of the Golden Rule" and even had a neon sign proclaiming "Pay What You Wish." The owners never turned away anyone hungry. In 1946 Clifford and his wife sold their cafeteria to their children so they could devote all their energies to "Meals for Millions" and their distribution of food to starving and malnourished humanity. Their Christian philosophy was manifest in a portion of the basement of the cafeteria called "The Garden." In the garden a life-sized figure of Christ knelt in prayer in Gethsemane. This sculpture by Marshall Lakey was an interpretation of artist Heinrich Hoffmann's picture.

With this witness by Clifton's Cafeteria, it is fitting that a devout Christian lady was privileged to have lunch with the Lord in Clifton's Cafeteria. She said the Lord appeared in disguise as a business man, dressed in a suit. As they chatted and supped together, she said the Lord enveloped them with an invisible shield so the other diners didn't notice or interrupt her visitation. The one significant detail of their meal together that impressed this lady was that the Lord did not drink any water until the ice had completely melted in His glass. Because of the sacredness of her encounter with the Lord she did not seek any public account of her visitation experience. "Behold, I am the Lord, the God of all flesh: is there any thing too hard for me?" (Jer 32:27). "If any man hear my voice and open the door, I will come in and sup with him." In this instance, His promise was literal.

Rev 11:3 speaks of the "two witnesses" and their prophecy before the return of the Lord at His second coming. At the California headquarters of the *Christ at the Door Ministry*, one afternoon two teenagers came to the door selling magazine subscriptions. After their conversation, as they were leaving, another member of the headquarters overheard one teenager make a remark to his companion that helped the member realize that the teenagers were no doubt messengers of God in disguise. "Is any thing too hard for the Lord?" (Gen 18:14).

At a California mental hospital, the staff would gather together to discuss every new admittance – history, treatment, prognosis, etc. At certain times during these staff meetings, when an unusually difficult patient presented, the staff noted that a doctor would appear at the staff meeting who would go into detail explaining all the how, why and details of the new patient's history of mental illness. The staff relied on these explanations because they were always "right on the mark." The guest doctor would quietly excuse himself after his presentation and not be seen until he would suddenly appear at another staff meeting on behalf of another patient. The staff never questioned the doctor, who he was, or what his qualifications were. The staff sensed this doctor was either the Lord appearing in disguise, or a messenger sent by the Lord to show God's love for one of His sheep who had lost its way in life.

Hebrews 13:2 admonishes: "Be not forgetful to entertain strangers: for thereby some have entertained angels unawares." Angels can also appear in disguise. In 1974 the media reported over sixty reports of a mysterious bearded hitchhiker, clad in resplendent white, who would thumb a ride on the New York State Interstate. The handsome hiker would climb into the back seat, button the seat belt and engage the driver in conversation. The stranger would finally ask the driver if he believed in the Second Coming of Christ. When the driver would turn around to answer, the hitchhiker would be gone, but the seat belt would still be fastened. Reports of the same events occurred in Arkansas also in the mid-1970s. The same chain of events was repeated several years later on Texas interstates. In 1984 the same events happened in West Germany. In West Germany the hitchhiker identified himself as the Archangel Gabriel and predicted the date of

Doomsday. Not only is Jesus Christ at our door spiritually, materially, by dream, by vision, and in disguise, but angels also prepare us for His coming.

Sun Magazine, March 20, 2006, had a special section titled "Visions of Jesus prove End Times are here." The article relied on the research of the Crucible Institute, a prophecy think tank, and the project's leader, Dr. Colin Rankin, a theology professor in New York City. Rankin noted the apparitions in all parts of the United States followed a similar pattern. The person who experienced the vision would first be struck by a momentary stillness. In this stillness there might appear a distant glow; the person would react to a state of perfect relaxation or could be especially moved by a prayer. Next the presence of the Lord would be announced by a piercingly bright light, or a sweet smell similar to roses or incense, or there could be a low, musical hum. These physical precursors increased in intensity until the Lord appeared and spoke. Some saw Christ surrounded by flames and the sounds of warfare.

His message was that thousands of people would vanish without a trace – their sudden disappearance would be the beginning of the Rapture. Those caught up in the Rapture would have perfect humility and unbounded love for their neighbor. Those left to hear His message would be purified by the coming flames and judged on their ability to love and their willingness to accept the heaviest of burdens. Others saw the Lord appear in white robes against a backdrop of black smoke. The Lord said, "It has come to this – a globe-encompassing war that will leave no city untouched by the ravages of violence…Now, more than ever, it is our duty to work for peace, to remember peace and to hold peace as our ultimate eternal goal." To other visionaries Jesus appeared in His crucified body with the bloody wounds in his hands and feet of the crucifixion. He warned of the antichrist and admonished his listeners to walk in love and walk away from the false gospel that condemns.

To others, a radiant Christ, crowned in glory, delivered a promise of salvation saying, "Difficult days lie ahead, with war and disease, hunger and strife spreading rapidly across the world. Do not give in to despair, for your hope will never be more precious. You are closer to God than ever. Pray with your heart, lead others in prayer, and your salvation is guaranteed."

Some visionaries reported apparitions of Christ standing beside the Virgin Mary. Together they warned: "Prepare yourselves for terrible events, but know that your souls are safe once committed to your Heavenly Father. The agonies of the world are like the pains of youth growing into adulthood. Pray for peace and your pains will be healed." Jesus and Mary instructed this prayer to be prayed: "Heavenly Father, who shines always above us in love, elevate our hearts into Thy wisdom. Commend our souls to Thy loving hands. Bring our thoughts into Thy all-seeing holiness. Teach us the ways of gratitude in every action, and from every part of Thy creation. Amen."

The Lord and angels sent by Him come to our door directly and in disguise to see if we will invite Him into our lives.

CHURCH VISITATIONS

*E*xodus 40: 34: "Then a cloud covered the tent of the congregation, and the glory of the Lord filled the tabernacle."

The Detroit News, June 1, 1964, carried the news of a visitation of the Lord to a church. Spencer Campbell, Jr. a 16-year-old boy preacher, was preaching at a small church in the community of Quick, near Charleston, West Virginia. Pastor Campbell said he had his sermon prepared and his scripture chosen for the service. As he was listening to the choir, he saw the Lord open the back door of the church and walk into the church. Spencer said, "There was a very bright light coming from His face. I couldn't see His face because of the light, but I could see His robes and His hands, and the blood dripping out of His wounds. I told the congregation what I was seeing, and some of them saw it too." The pastor said that since the first vision, additional visions have occurred. He said, "It's usually Jesus I see, but I can never get a look at His face. The light is too bright." Note that the Lord appeared in his crucified body. Spencer said he has had visions of Christ on several occasions, but the visitation of the Lord coming to the back door of the church, opening it and entering has stirred a minor revival. At DuPont high school that Spencer attended, two schoolteachers and 200 students were converted.

A few years earlier, also in June, but in 1960, the Lord visited the Yucatan Mission Church in Central America. A grandson of the late

Emperor of Austria, Prince Adolph Friederich Welheim von Hapsburg was present in the congregation and happened to have his camera with him, so he took a picture of the Lord at his visitation. The Lord appeared in His resurrected body.

Marie Miller in the October 7, 1974, issue of *Midnight* magazine reported that on Good Friday of that year as the local priest in a small hamlet in southern France was celebrating mass with about 30 parishioners in the village church, he lifted the cloth off the chalice as usual. But the priest suddenly lifted his arms in surprise and admiration. After not moving for a few moments he suddenly exclaimed: "It's Jesus, it's Jesus. Come and see! It's Jesus." First, the assistant to the priest also saw the face of Jesus on the chalice. All the congregation came to the altar to see the miracle. The news of the apparition spread quickly and hordes of tourists as well as other believers soon came to also see. The bishop of the region said, "There is nothing impossible about it. If the Lord wants it, He can show Himself in a special way."

In the Old Testament when Solomon finished building the temple (1 Kings 8:10), the glory of the Lord so filled the house of the Lord that the priests could not stand to minister because the glory of the Lord was so intense. Colossians 2:9 tells us that "in Him dwelleth all the fullness of the Godhead bodily." That is, when Jesus is invited into our home and/or into our life, He brings the same glory to us that was manifested in the Old Testament temple. 1st Corinthians 6:19 explains that with the coming of Jesus, He has hid His temple in us, so when Jesus visits us, He brings the glory of the Lord to us just as in the Old Testament when the glory of the Lord resided first in the tent of the congregation and later in the temple at Jerusalem.

We need to recognize there are three churches. All believers are a part of the universal church composed of all believers. The Apostles Creed calls this universal church the holy catholic church. The second church is the denominational church with each denomination having its own doctrine and its own creed. The second church is composed of believers from Eastern and Western Catholic to Pentecostal and from major denominations to independent community churches. The third church is the church in the home. Jesus said, "Where two or three are gathered together in my name, there am I in the midst of them" (Mt 18:20). Jesus also said, "But thou, when thou prayest, enter into thy closet, and when thou hast shut thy door, pray to thy Father which is in secret; and thy Father which seeth in secret shall reward thee openly" (Mt 6:6). Every believer, single or married, has a church in his home. He/she can prepare for the visitation of the Lord in their home.

We suggest a daily home church schedule to help family members prepare for a closer walk with the Lord. Both Daniel (6:10) "he kneeled upon his knees three times a day, and prayed, and gave thanks before his God" and David (Psalm 55:17) "Evening, and morning, and at noon, will I pray, and cry aloud; and He shall hear my voice" based their relationship with God on the daily discipline of prayer three times a day. Family devotions every evening; saying grace at each meal; a family altar with the Lord's picture and an open Bible; a place setting for the Lord at the head of the table to symbolize accepting His Presence as the head of the house are all disciplines a family can use to establish the home Sunday school and home church. Love shown by all members of the family allows the Lord's love to be felt in the family.

Catholic professor of catechetics, Christiane Brusselmans, in 1970 wrote *A Parent's Guide: Religion for Little Children*. She makes the point that parents must realize their home is the first and primary church and Sunday school for their children by stating:

> "Christian families are not only a miniature of the church but they constitute the church as the living cells in which the life of Christ exists...It is in the home that parents start shaping the children's basic attitudes to joyful and meaningful participation in the official liturgy of the church." (p 88). "In the first place, nothing can substitute for the religious experience and witness that children encounter in their family situation.

For pre-school children, the die is cast with parents, their first catechists, and the home – (the child's) first and most important religious classroom." (p 153).

A time for worship and prayer is important in the home church but Brusselmans points out that the way a child is loved in the home is more important than schedule, form and doctrine. Parents cannot shift their responsibility to the church to bring up a child in the faith of their church – it begins at home. "Religious psychology shows that religion is located in a person's deep emotions and that it is the result of the way in which he or she was socialized by the adults who cared for him or her as a child....A child's personal concept of God is shaped by the earliest experiences with both parents, for they are visible signs and symbols of God."

So whether we want to have a home church is not the question. The home is a church and Sunday school whether we like it or not. The child learns to pray by seeing their parents pray. Children learn about God, Christ and the Holy Spirit by hopefully experiencing love in the home. They are taught the basics of faith by seeing how their parents live and treat each other.

Parents can invite the Lord through their door by the way they lead their daily lives. Daily prayer and worship in the home church can continue in the denominational week-end church of their choice. Paul preaches: "When ye come together, every one of you hath a psalm, hath a doctrine, hath a tongue, hath a revelation, hath an interpretation. Let all things be done unto edifying" (1st Cor 14.26). In other words, as a result of the active home church, everyone has something to bring to the Sunday denominational church. We have given three unusual examples of Christ visiting week-end churches. But if He is invited, He will come through the door and reside in every home church every day.

Roger Frederickson, a Baptist minister and lecturer in Wichita, Kansas, has stated that too often pastors don't want their membership too involved at home because it could mean a loss of some of their power and prestige. But the stronger the home church, the stronger the week-end church. Ministers, priests, and rabbis can help parents be adequate home pastors to their children. Brusselmans wrote her book to dispel the notion that parents can just send their children to confirmation classes and Sunday school to do the work parents should have done at home.

Brusselmans' 1970s thesis has been proven by the 2014 fourth wave of the National Study of Youth and Religion. The first wave of the comprehensive national study was conducted in 2002-2003 among teens age 13 to 17 and their parents. Now these teens are age 24 to 29. Christian Smith, lead researcher for the study and a sociologist at the University of Notre Dame in Indiana, found in 2014 that 82 percent of children who were raised by parents who talked about faith at home, attached great importance to their beliefs, and were active in their congregations were religiously active as young adults. In contrast just one percent of teens age 15 to 17 raised by parents who attached little importance to religion were highly religious in their mid to late twenties. In comparing factors such as youth ministry, clergy, service projects and even religious schools, Smith said nothing else comes remotely close to matching the influence of mothers and fathers who practice what they preach and preach what they practice. Jesus Christ is at the door of families because He loves us – parents and children. What better way to worship Him every day than in the way we express our love for Him and for one another.

GOD VISITATIONS

Can we be visited by God? Genesis tells the story of Jacob who wrestled with an angel at Peniel. And Jacob said, "for I have seen God face to face, and my life is preserved" (Gen 32:30). Job proclaimed: "I have heard of thee by the hearing of the ear; but now mine eye seeth thee" (Job 42:5). Isaiah proclaimed: "for mine eyes have seen the King, the Lord of hosts" (Isaiah 6:5). Mt 5:8 promises: "Blessed are the pure in heart: for they shall see God."

In the Old Testament we have the record of many experiences of the visitation of God to man. In Genesis 17:1 we read that God visited Abram to be seen. "And when Abram was ninety years old and nine, the Lord appeared to Abram, and said unto him, 'I am the Almighty God: walk before me, and be thou perfect.'" In the 18th chapter of Genesis we read that God appeared unto Abraham in the plains of Mamre in disguise as three strangers. Abraham saw and heard God in disguise. God called Moses by having the angel of the Lord appear unto Moses as a flame of fire out of the midst of a burning bush. Moses knew his people would want to know what phase of God had spoken to him, so Moses asked God his name. God said, "Thus shalt thou say unto the children of Israel, 'I AM hath sent me unto you'" (Ex 3:14). "And the Lord spake unto Moses face to face as a man speaketh unto his friend" (Ex 33:11).

Exodus records that Moses, Aaron, Nadab, Abihu, and 70 of the elders were called up to sup with God. We read, "And they saw the

God of Israel: and there was under His feet as it were a paved work of a sapphire stone, and as it were the body of heaven in His clearness. And upon the nobles of the children of Israel He laid not His hand: also they saw God, and did eat and drink" (Ex 24:10).

Joshua saw God manifested as the captain of the host of the Lord (5:14). Abram saw Melchizadek, priest of the most high God (Gen 14:18). Daniel 7:9,10 describes seeing God as the Ancient of Days: "I beheld till the thrones were cast down, and the Ancient of Days did sit, whose garment was white as snow, and the hair of his head like the pure wool; His throne was like the fiery flame, and His wheels as burning fire. A fiery stream issued and came forth from before Him; thousand thousands ministered unto Him, and ten thousand times ten thousand stood before Him." Isaiah said, "In the year that king Uzziah died, I saw the Lord seated on a throne, high and exalted, and the train of his robe filled the temple" (6:1). Ezekiel gives a lengthy description of the four cherubims that accompany God and adds, "This was the appearance of the likeness of the glory of the Lord. And when I saw it, I fell face down, and I heard the voice of one speaking" (1:28). We know that Job saw God for he said to God, "I have heard of thee by the hearing of the ear; but now mine eye seeth thee. Wherefore I abhor myself, and repent in dust and ashes" (42:5-6).

We wish to present some modern day visitations of God to man that your faith might be strengthened that either God, Jesus, or the Holy Spirit may visit and come to your door. On August 22, 1741 the composer George Frederick Handel shut himself in his study and was inspired to begin working on his composition, the Messiah. His fortunes and health were at low ebb, but his inspiration gave him incredible energy and he practically worked around the clock and barely touched food brought to him. The composition was written in only 24 days. One day during composing, a servant found Handel slumped across his music and his head was buried in his arms. The servant of course wanted to know what happened. Handel looked up and his cheeks were streaked from tears. Handel replied in awe, "I did think I did see all heaven before me and the great God Himself."

Kenneth Hagin, a well known evangelist, tells his experience of God indicating his Presence as a glory cloud in his pamphlet titled *I Went to Hell*. Kenneth relates that after being bedfast as a child for 16 months he was about to die on August 16, 1933. He was not yet 16 but his temperature had risen to 106 degrees on a hot August day. Kenneth asked his younger brother to get his mother as he wanted to tell her goodbye before he died. After Kenneth's younger brother left the room, the whole room became bright with the glory of God. In the brilliant presence of God, Kenneth left his material body and started toward heaven. By this time Kenneth's mother was about to enter Kenneth's room when she looked and noticed the room was full of something like a thick fog. She realized the presence of God was in the room so she retreated from the room and went into an adjoining room to pray. Kenneth's grandmother heard Kenneth was dying so she tried to run through the door to see Kenneth. As she tried to run through the door, she bounced off of the glory of God. Not realizing what was happening, the grandmother backed up to gain momentum and tried to run into the room again, but bounced off the glory of God a second time. After a third failure to enter the room she took time to look into the room and said, "I can't see. The room is filled with something like a fog or a while cloud. I can't see the bed. I can't see Kenneth. I can't see into the room, and I can't get in there."

Kenneth's mother by this time saw what was happening to Grandma so she suggested she wait. Grandma agreed so they both prayed. After about 10 minutes they saw the fog was lifting and after the last wisp of the glory cloud of God was gone, they entered the room. Kenneth opened his eyes and told them he wasn't going to die because Jesus visited him and said, "Go back; go back; go back to the earth; your work is not done." God manifested as a glory cloud to Kenneth Hagin.

In the Old Testament God made His presence known as the Pillar of cloud by day and the Pillar of fire by night. When Jesus was resurrected a cloud received him out of their sight (Acts 1:9-11). In the following account of a visitation of God, notice the presence of God as a cloud, the presence of the Lord as the Sword of the Lord, and the Holy Spirit in the form of a dove. In June, 1982 after seeking to know the Lord for 22 years, a man was in his apartment in the state of Louisiana. Suddenly he heard a sound coming from behind him and slightly to his left. When he turned he saw a small cloud which was being driven right to him by a light wind. He watched the cloud come over him and from the cloud he saw the hand of God emerge and touch his head.

Because he knew that God was touching his life, he started praying and felt God prick his heart. He repented and prayed that he might be forgiven his sins. He told his wife his experience and she took him to her church that night where he was baptized. The next day as he was praying on his knees, he became aware of the sword of the Lord outside his chest. Next, he felt the hand of God inside his body raise him up. When he stood up he was impressed to look outside his back door. Again a cloud was driven right to him by a light wind and the cloud descended right over his head and took the form of a dove. After this visitation of God, this Christian man has felt the presence of God, the Lord and the Holy Spirit with him ever since in his daily life.

Andrew C. Sorelle, Jr. told his visitation by God in the February, 1966 issue of *Guidepost* magazine. In 1944 Andrew was a pilot in the 48th Fighter Group of the 9th Air Force. His unit was one of the first to be moved to Normandy after the invasion of France in World War II. His fighter group flew from a steel matted flying strip hastily laid down in the midst of the Normandy apple orchards and hedgerows. In early July, Andrew was one of four pilots sent to fly their Thunderbolts to attack a column of retreating German trucks. The weather was so bad the pilots had to fly low just under the cloud ceiling. Soon they came over a hill and found the enemy trucks and equipment on the highway right below them. By the time they circled and returned to attack, the enemy had time to mount their guns on each side of the

The Gospel of Visitation

road and the planes had to fly through their crossfire. Andrew felt a heavy jolt to his plane. He saw that a German 88-MM shell had ripped a three foot hole through his left wing. A series of miracles began. First, the shell which was fused to explode on contact did not explode and only cut the aileron cable. But the aileron is the tab on the trailing edge of each wing which gives the pilot 90 percent of the control of the plane. As a result of his plane being hit the left wing aileron fell off the Thunderbolt and the right aileron was flopping out of control.

Andrew knew the plane would nose down, barrel-roll to the left and crash. The roll started just 200 feet from the ground. Next the second miracle occurred. Instead of barrel-rolling to the left and nosing into a crash, the plane instead made a steep climbing turn to the right, just the maneuver Andrew needed to return to his airstrip. His plane miraculously flew into the overcast and leveled out. Andrew looked at his control stick, which was making wild circular movements. His instruments were gone. With the plane level, Andrew knew he had just enough time to bail out. He threw open the canopy and started to bail out but a third miracle occurred. He was physically and mysteriously held from jumping out. So he sat back down in the plane and buckled up again. Suddenly his plane broke out of the overcast and he saw his airstrip to his right. The only control he had left was the tail rudder, so he used the rudder to do a flat skid. He cut the throttle and the plane hit at the beginning of the temporary matted runway. Going 170 miles an hour, he bounced down the runway and came to a stop in the mud at the end of the runway.

When Andrew turned off the plane's ignition switch he felt a supernatural hush in the cockpit. He sat quietly in silence and God became real. Audibly Andrew heard five clear words. God said, "I have saved your life." Andrew knew he was in the indescribable presence of God. He knew God had miraculously controlled events and guided the crippled plane on its return when aerodynamically it was impossible. Andrew was a changed man from that time forward because of God's direct and personal visitation.

Many times we read a story and don't realize until later that we were given the details of a visitation of God. For example, in the September 1983 issue of the *Ladies Home Journal* author Sherry Cohen wrote the article titled "Love on Trial," the story of Christina, the wife of John DeLorean. We remember John DeLorean was arrested and implicated in drug trafficking reportedly to try and save his failing sports-car factory and business. Christina was raised in a major religious Christian faith, but all her life she said she was seeking something spiritual, something her church didn't seem to provide. She felt God would fill her void if she could somehow reach Him. Her sister became a born-again Christian four years earlier and had shared her new found relationship with God with her sister. Christina had a premonition of trouble and felt it would take a "major zap" to help her really reach the relationship she wanted with God.

The premonition materialized with the arrest of her husband. By the third night alone after her husband's arrest, Christina was so heartbroken and scared that she kept her eleven-year-old son and her five-year-old daughter in bed with her. She held her children close to her but even so, she was sobbing uncontrollably. She realized this was frightening her children so she prayed to God, "Please let me stop. Please control me. Please let me not scare these innocent babies." God answered her prayer. She was able to stop sobbing and she felt a huge weight being lifted from her. She felt calm and at peace. She felt safe. The next night she started sobbing again and again her prayer was answered. The third night, she again had the same experience of sobbing, praying and feeling God's peace. Christina said, "This is the funny part. I recognized God—I wasn't scared or in awe or struck dumb. It was as if He was my true friend, speaking to me in my own language. I could hear Him say, 'Hey, cut it out, kid. Everything will be cool. Have faith; it really will be okay.'" Christina said God felt familiar, not a gigantic, distant presence. As her friends deserted her because of her husband's arrest Christina realized God was her greatest friend. Her visitation and His continuing presence helped her weather the storm in her life.

The famous basketball coach Phil Jackson's latest book (with Hugh Delehanty) is *Eleven Rings: The Soul of Success* (2013, Penguin Press). This former basketball coach of the Bulls and Lakers tells a visitation experience when he was about eleven or twelve years old. Phil's father was a minister and preached Sunday mornings. Phil's mother was also a minister and preached Sunday evenings. In addition to church twice on Sunday, Phil attended midweek services. His parents had devotions every morning before breakfast and Phil and his siblings often memorized Bible verses at night. His parents were part of the Pentecostal movement with its fundamental faith that one found salvation by connecting directly with the Holy Spirit. When Phil was about eleven his mother told him it was time for him to seek the infilling of the Holy Spirit. The baptism of the Holy Spirit was manifest by speaking in tongues.

Phil had a number of curious health issues as a child. About two years of age Phil developed a large growth on his throat that had to be treated with penicillin before it eventually went way. This experience caused Phil to grow up feeling that there was something about him that wasn't quite right. When he entered first grade Phil was diagnosed with a heart murmur and had to avoid physical activity for a whole year. This experience certainly didn't help. When he was about eleven or twelve Phil was sick again battling a high fever. Phil recalls:

> "I was sleeping fitfully, when all of a sudden I heard a roar, like the sound of a railroad train, building and building until it grew so loud I thought the train was going to burst into my bedroom. The sensation was completely overpowering, but for some reason I wasn't frightened. As the noise kept getting louder, I felt a powerful surge of energy radiating through my body that was much stronger and more all consuming than anything I'd ever experienced before. I don't know where this power came from, but I awoke the next day feeling strong and confident and brimming with energy. The fever was gone, and

after that my health improved dramatically and I rarely got colds or flu. However, the primary impact of this spontaneous experience was psychological, not physical. After that night I had a greater belief in myself and a quiet faith that everything was going to work out for the best. I also seemed to be able to tap into a new source of energy within myself that I hadn't sensed before" (p 48).

Phil had seen manifestations of the Holy Spirit by speaking in tongues but of course he didn't realize he had a visitation by God manifested as a powerful wind. 1 Kings 19:11 tells of Elijah's experience of the Lord passing by as a great and strong wind. Phil writes: "I've always wondered where that power came from and whether I could learn how to tap into it on my own..." Phil tells of his spiritual journey to find that power again. Phil's parents were praying for him to receive his spiritual gift. They thought it would be the Holy Spirit. God decided to visit Himself. "The effectual fervent prayer of a righteous man availeth much" (James 5:16).

Paula Rinehart in *Strong Women – Soft Hearts* (2001, Thomas Nelson) relates that while serving a three-month internship at a county drug and alcohol facility, the doctor in charge asked her to talk to a woman who was distraught because in addition to battling her own cocaine addiction her roommate had just tried to commit suicide. Paula tried to console her but her words weren't touching the patient. Not knowing what else to do, Paula asked the patient if she could pray for her. The patient replied, "Oh would you please?" After a simple prayer, the patient who had been shaking and distraught became quiet and peaceful. Paula asked what had happened as she prayed. The patient replied, "I saw God on His throne. And He asked me to sit in His lap. Then He said, 'There now, Sybil, you will be OK. You will be OK.'"

God can visit; Jesus can visit; the Holy Spirit can visit.

Visitations of the Living Word of God using the Written Word of God

The book of Revelation, chapter 3 verse 20 gives us the promise that Jesus wishes to visit ever one of His creation. Here is His promise: "Behold, I stand at the door and knock: if any man hear my voice, and open the door, I will come in to him, and will sup with him, and he with Me." When Jesus visits us we call that blessed experience a visitation. But when Jesus promises to sup with us that means He wishes to dine with us daily, to live with us daily. John 14:23 explains that not only can we have a living fellowship with the Lord, but also with His Father; "If a man love me, he will keep my words; and my Father will love him, and we will come unto him, and make our abode with Him." This is heavenly living while still on the earth; fellowship with Jesus and God daily. Peter calls this way of living being established in present day truth. The stories we read in the bible of men and women experiencing God in their lives can be present day experiences for us. The written Word of God can help lead us to the Living Word of God, Jesus Christ.

Some Christians worship the Bible, the book about the Lord, instead of letting the Bible lead us to worship of the Lord. For example, a number of years ago I listened to a radio preacher who read these words: "Search the scriptures; for in them ye have eternal life." That is what the fundamental preacher wished the Bible said. What the bible actually says in John 5:39-40 is this: "Search the scriptures;

for in them ye THINK ye have eternal life: and they are they which testify of me. And ye will not come to me, that ye might have life." Jesus does not want us to worship the book about Him. He wishes us to use the Bible to lead us to His living presence. The written Word of God points to the Living Word of God.

Albert Mohler, Jr. in his book *Desire and Deceit: The Real Cost of the New Sexual Tolerance* (2008, Multnomah) states (p 76): "We can speak only because we are confident that the one sovereign God and Lord has revealed Himself and His will in an inerrant and authoritative Scripture." This theology limits the activity of God to what He has done in the past. The Bible, the written Word of God, prepares us to live with Jesus Christ, the living Word of God.

Second Timothy has two instructions for us in the use of the Bible. Second Timothy 2:15 tells us: "Study to shew thyself approved unto God, a workman that needeth not to be ashamed, rightly dividing the word of truth." Why does the Bible need to be divided? Theologians point to conflicts between different writers in the Bible. Who better to help us rightly divide the truth from the errors in the Bible than the Lord himself. Second Timothy 3:15 also tells us: "All scripture is given by inspiration of God, and is profitable for doctrine, for reproof, for correction, for instruction in righteousness: That the man of God may be perfect, thoroughly furnished unto all good works." The written Word of God points to the Living Word of God. The Bible from Genesis to Revelation is a record of God's visitations to man.

Hebrews admonishes: "See that ye refuse not Him that speaketh. For if they escaped not who refused Him that spake on earth, much more shalt not we escape, if we turn away from Him that speaketh from heaven" (12:25). The Bible then helps prepare us to look beyond the record ABOUT Jesus Christ so we can experience the PRESENCE of Jesus Christ when we have the blessing of His visitation. As the Lord said to Abraham (18:14): "Is any thing too hard for the Lord." Second Peter 1:12 admonishes us to be established in present day truth. Be aware of how the living Word of God is revealing His truth in our day and age. One way to be established in the present day truth is to learn from those who have suffered horrible traffic accidents and died and gone to heaven before being revived and returned to life. Because they have seen the Lord in heaven, we can learn from their visits with the Lord. Richard Sigmund in his book *My Time in Heaven: A True story of dying and coming back* (2010, Whitaker House) helps us understand the relation between the written Word of God and the living Word of God. He writes (p 85), "We often think that what is contained in the Word is the sum total of what God will do for us, but it is not. In a sense, God limited Himself when He recorded His Word for us. He didn't include all that He is and all that He can do, because He is infinite. While we are on earth, we cannot comprehend or receive what He has planned for us ultimately."

As a result of his heavenly visit, Richard testifies: "Every day, I hear the audible voice of God in some manner. I see the angels of God. And I have seen Jesus on numerous occasions. In revival meetings, the angels are visible to me. The cloud of glory is visible to me" (p 130). During his heavenly visit, the Lord explained to Richard about the written Word of God:

> "For centuries, men have tried to interpret My Word. Some were correct, in as much light as they had. Some were wrong, and some of them were sent by the evil one to lead my Father's creation astray. From the day that My grace was extended to redeem creation, the evil one has tried to steal it from My hands. But until the day that I will soon return, that which My Father had committed to Me will not be taken from Me. I have worked to make salvation available to all....Soon, I will take the heavenly armies that you have witnessed, along with these elders that are here, and go to get My people. It will be the happiest time of all eternity" (p 125-126).

The living Word of God, our Lord Jesus Christ, can speak directly to us if we are privileged to have a direct visitation. But the Lord can also speak to us by using the written Word of God. For example: Mrs. W was suffering and sick. Doctors gave some help but were unable to affect a cure. She knew her healing would have to come from God. She prayed daily and asked the Lord if it was His will to heal her. One day as she was reading the book of Proverbs in the Old Testament she came across a passage in the middle of a sentence: "Thy expectation shall not be cut off." The lord just lifted that passage out of Proverbs 24:14 to assure her he would heal her. Next she asked to know when it was His time to heal and the Lord gave her a time – day and hour. At the appointed time she knelt beside her bed in prayer. Soon the Lord appeared on the other side of the bed. He extended his hand to her and she reached to touch Him. As she touched His hand, she felt the power of His touch and she felt the electricity of His power go through her body and she was healed by the power of His presence. The living Word of God first spoke by highlighting a passage in the written Word of God. Next the living Word of God spoke directly and gave a time when he would appear. Finally the living Word of God appeared in a physical body she could touch when He healed her.

Another example of the Lord speaking by using His written Word: Mrs. H was discouraged and despondent. As she prayed for healing and strength the Lord said, "Ephesians 3:13." She went to her Bible and read, "Wherefore I desire that ye faint not at my tribulations for you, which is your glory." Then she knew the Lord was giving her strength to overcome her depression.

For an example of the living Word of God explaining the written Word of God, we have the visitation of Mrs. B. Her visitation is also an example of visitations by voice – the Lord visiting by speaking to us. As a young girl in high school she saved her money to be able to go to Bible College. The summer before school was to begin, her father became sick and he asked her permission to use her college savings to pay his medical bills. Of course she had to help her father; but how could she go to school with her tuition money spent? As she prayed about her problem, she distinctly heard the Lord say, "Daughter, You go; I'll see you through." She enrolled in faith; secured a part-time job and worked her way through Bible College. As she was nearing graduation she was dating two Christian young men. She naturally was wondering which young man was God's choice for her to marry. She began to have more feelings for one of the young men. She asked God if this feeling was revealing God's choice of husband for her. The Lord again spoke audibly, "Daughter, this is my choice for thee." After graduation and marriage to her pastor husband, the years rolled by. She was busy with family and all the activities of a pastor's wife. One day she recognized that her prayer time was being neglected. Wondering how to put her prayer life back to its prominent place she audibly called out one day, "Lord, when can I have some time just with you?" The Lord answered audibly, "How about 5:00 in the morning?"

She wondered how she could maintain her busy schedule with less sleep. But the Lord had answered her prayer. Knowing that God speaks twice, she asked God that if this was His voice would He please speak twice and confirm His instruction by waking her up at 5:00 himself. Sure enough at 5:00 the next morning she awoke thinking that she had just heard her alarm ring. Mrs. B loved her Bible, so after her initial 5:00 prayer on her knees, she sat and read a Bible passage. After reading she felt the Lord's presence just behind and to her right as she sat in her chair. The Lord gave a private exposition of the passage she had just read, amplifying and explaining in depth what the words had merely introduced. This continued for each daily 5:00 hour of prayer. She said it was like having a private tutor for an hour every morning. Each morning the Lord would awaken her at 5:00, always in a slightly different way. Her private visitation of the Lord each morning was so refreshing that His presence more than compensated for the sleep she missed.

Another example of the Living Word of God using the Written Word of God.

J.D. had the gift of communing with the Lord; he also enjoyed reading Christian books as well as the Bible. One evening he had a dream where the Lord appeared with a Bible in His hand. The Lord said, "This book is all you need to read to know how to follow me."

Some Christians have asked the Living Word of God to guide them and inspire them by using the Written Word of God. They take their Bible and by prayer ask the Lord to open the Bible to the book He wants and then guiding their finger to the verse on the page he wishes to use to speak/ instruct/inspire.

Dr. Reggie Anderson tells the true story of his NDE and healing encounters with the hereafter in *Appointments with Heaven* (2013, Tyndale, Momentum). In the final notes of his amazing heaven visitation he writes (p311): "Though God has sometimes enabled me to peer beyond the veil separating this world from the next, my greatest insights into heaven come from a resource that is just as available to you as it is to me: Scripture."

Evangelist David E. Taylor in *Face-to-Face Appearances from Jesus: The Ultimate Intimacy* (Destiny Image Publishers, 2009) supports the fact that we can have an intimate relationship with the living Word of God giving proof from the Bible, the written Word of God. He writes (p 69-70):

> "I thought it important to destroy the ungodly lies and myths concerning seeing Jesus face-to-face that exist in the Church today. There are lots of religious people who will try to discourage you from believing that these types of experiences with God are possible, or that you can have a relationship with Him of this magnitude. People who have had face-to-face encounters in dreams with the Lord Jesus have come to me and shared the responses and attitudes they've experienced from some saints. After a young man shared about a visitation

he had from the Lord, his church told him that God doesn't do that today! In fact they told him that the visitation was from Satan. How ignorant and how horrible this is on their part. May God forgive them."

EVIL VISITATIONS

We know visitations from God prepared for the birth of our Lord when He incarnated. Mary was visited by the angel Gabriel and told she would give birth to Jesus (Lk 1:26). Joseph was visited by the angel of the Lord in a dream and told to take Mary as his bride even though she was pregnant, because her pregnancy was by the Holy Ghost (Mt 1:20). After the birth of Jesus, Joseph was again visited by an angel of the Lord in a dream and told to flee to Egypt (Mt 2:13). Joseph was again visited by an angel of the Lord in a dream and told when it was safe to return to Nazareth (Mt 2:22).

The first visitation Jesus had as an adult that we have record of occurred when Jesus was baptized by John. After Jesus came out of the water, the scriptures tell us "Lo, the heavens were opened unto Him, and He saw the Spirit of God descending like a dove, and lighted upon Him; and lo, a voice from heaven, saying, 'This is my beloved Son, in whom I am well pleased'" (Mt 3:17). The book of Matthew tells us that just as soon as Jesus was visited by God, Jesus was led by the spirit to go into the wilderness to be tempted by Satan. Satan tempted while Jesus fasted forty days and forty nights. After Satan departed Jesus had another visitation from God—angels of God who came and ministered unto Him. Note the progression of the three visitations—first God, then Satan, and then God again.

In looking forward to our visitation from God we need to realize that if Jesus, the son of God, had to withstand the visitation of Satan, we must also be aware of evil visitations as well. James explains that every man is tempted but "let no man say when he is tempted, I am tempted of God" (1:14). The book of Job explains that God allows the temptation, but the devil does the tempting. To repeat, in helping you become aware that God has a plan to visit his creation, and helping you see the mercy of His plan so you can prepare for this blessing, we must also help you be aware that there can be evil visitations.

Some Christians are so afraid of a possible visitation of the devil they make the mistake of rejecting all visitations and miss the blessing of visitations from the Lord. Paul told the Thessalonian church to "Quench not the spirit. Despise not prophesying. Prove all things; hold fast that which is good. Abstain from all appearance of evil" (1 Thess 5:19). James recognized the possibility of visitations from both good and evil when he wrote: "Resist the devil, and he will flee from you. Draw night to God, and He will draw nigh to you" (4:7). Paul wrote to the Ephesians: "We wrestle not against flesh and blood, but against principalities, against powers, against the rulers of the darkness of this world, against spiritual wickedness in high places. Wherefore take unto you the whole armor of God that you may be able to withstand in the evil day, and having done all, to stand" (Eph: 6:12-13). Jesus recognized the battle between good and evil when he said, "...he that endureth unto the end shall be saved" (Mt 10:22).

As we prepare for our visitation from the Lord, our job is to be able to discern the true from the false, the good from the bad, entertain a visitation from God, and reject a visitation from the devil. How can we discern?

The Bible lists ways we can "prove all things; hold fast that which is good" to use Paul's advice to the Thessalonians. Jesus gave us one guide: "By their fruits ye shall know them" (Mt 7:20). People who have the privilege of receiving a visitation of Christ speak of the light around him and His love which engulfs them. People who have contacted evil beings speak of the horror, fear and terror. By their fruits ye shall know them. Is there love or fear with the presence of the spirit? Paul gives the same advice to the Ephesians (5:9-11): "For the fruit of the Spirit is in all goodness and righteousness and truth: Proving what is acceptable unto the Lord. And have no fellowship with the unfruitful works of darkness, but rather reprove them."

Another guide is found in Ist John 4:1. "Beloved, believe not every spirit, but try the spirits whether they are of God....Hereby know ye the Spirit of God: Every spirit that confesseth that Jesus Christ is come in the flesh is of God: And every spirit that confesseth not that Jesus Christ is come in the flesh is not of God." This same guide is found in Paul's first letter to the Corinthians (12:3,4): "...no man speaking by the Spirit of God calleth Jesus accursed; and that no man can say that Jesus is the Lord, but by the Holy Ghost." If unsure, a Christian can simply ask a spirit, "Do you come in the name of the Lord?"

A rule to determine if a prophet's prophesy is true or false is found in the 18th chapter of Deuteronomy, verse 22. "When a prophet speaketh in the name of the Lord, if the thing follow not, nor come to pass, that is the thing which the Lord hath not spoken, but the prophet hath spoken it presumptuously. thou shalt not be afraid of him."

John White in 1990 wrote *The Meeting of Science and Spirit*. John had a near death experience when he drowned as a teenager. After military service he was the director of education of the Institute of Noetic Sciences which was founded by Apollo 14 astronaut Edgar Mitchell. He had an additional spontaneous mystical experience in 1963. In his book he recognizes that "the human race has been uplifted by words of wisdom originating, it seems, from levels of existence beyond the human which are inhabited by more highly evolved beings who are compassionately concerned for us and whose existence is, the communications say, inextricably entwined with our own." Who are these beings? He names "angels, archangels, devas, ascended masters and mahatmas, spirit guides, exusiai, cherubim, seraphim, extraterrestrials, metaterrestrials, ultraphysicals, Space Brothers, and so on" (p 173). He calls all of these "sources of channeled communications." Because of his near death experience and spontaneous mystical experience, he writes about the messenger work of angels and archangels and sources of channeled communications. His book helps us realize that there is visitation by many lesser channels.

White realizes these communications can come from the light or the dark, from good sources or evil sources. He devotes several pages to "consider in testing the nature, orientation, and spiritual quality of channeled communications." His first advice: "Are the communications compatible with the body of scientific knowledge?" His second point of advice: "Are the communications comparable with the teachings of the world's major religions and spiritual traditions?"

One type of channeled communication is mentioned in the Bible. The Bible calls this lower type of visitation "familiar spirits" Leviticus (19:31). We are admonished: "Regard not them that have familiar spirits, neither seek after wizards, to be defiled by them; I am the Lord your God." God is asking, "Why communicate with a familiar spirit when you can communicate with Me?" The Lord warned: "And the soul that turneth after such as have familiar spirits, and after wizards, to go a whoring after them, I will even set my face against that soul, and will cut him off from among his people. Sanctify yourselves therefore, and be ye holy: for I am the Lord your God" (Lev. 20:6, 7). The penalty for those who manifested a familiar spirit was to be put to death (Lev. 20:27). White helps us realize there are many types of communication available from the spiritual realm. But Christians can say with Joshua, "As for me and my house, we will serve the Lord" (24:15). We can add to the declaration of Joshua and say, "As for me and my house we will seek to communicate only with the Lord."

To continue the story of familiar spirits, we remember the predicament of Saul who was king and was terrified at the army of the Philistines that he faced. The Lord would not answer Saul's prayers for guidance so in desperation Saul found a woman with a familiar spirit who had escaped being put to death by his own decree. Saul persuaded the medium he would not put her to death for using her ability to bring back Samuel from the dead. When Samuel spoke he reminded Saul that his disobedience of the Lord was the reason the Lord would not answer him. Samuel said Saul and his army would be defeated by the Philistines. Saul's attempt to circumvent the Lord's proper channel of communication came to naught. He was defeated in battle.

The *National Enquirer* in 1976 gave an example of an evil visitation. Clifton Davis, a TV actor of that period, said when he was sixteen, he became so lonely that he lost faith in God. He decided to ask Satan to help him so he called out, "Satan, if you are real, appear to me." Satan did appear and brought so much terror with him that Davis became so scared that he called upon the name of the Lord to release him from the devil. The Lord answered his prayer; Satan left, and Davis's faith was restored. Another example of an evil visitation: Ray Oller, a doctor of chiropractic, was practicing in Ohio when the devil appeared to him. Ray said the devil was red in color and had horns and hoofs just as the devil is often depicted. The devil had a proposition for Ray. The devil promised Ray that he could have anything he wanted for seven years, if at the end of those seven years he could have his soul. Ray just laughed and told the devil he would be foolish to accept such a proposition. What is interesting is that at the end of seven years Ray moved to California, met Dr. A. Stanley Rogers and took the training to be a white light doctor.

Scott Peck, M.D. in *People of the Lie: The Hope for Healing Human Evil* (1983, Touchstone) believes "There are only two states of being: submission to God and goodness or the refusal to submit to anything beyond one's own will— which refusal automatically enslaves one to the forces of evil. We must ultimately belong either to God or the devil. This paradox was, of course, expressed by Christ when He said, 'Whosoever will save his life shall lose it. And whosoever shall lose his life, for my sake, shall find it'" (p 83). Peck quotes C.S. Lewis who said "There is no neutral ground in the universe; every square inch, every split second is claimed by God and counterclaimed by Satan." Jesus had to say to Satan, "Get thee hence, Satan (Mt 4:10) and "Get thee behind me, Satan (Mt 16:23). With His presence and power we can do the same.

The ultimate evil visitation Christians want to avoid is to meet Satan in Hell. The Lord in 1976 visited Mary K. Baxter and told her that she was chosen for a special assignment. He was going to reveal to Mary the reality of hell, "that many may be saved, many will repent of their evil ways before it is too late. Your soul will be taken out of your body, by me the Lord Jesus Christ and transmitted into hell and other places that I want you to see. I will also show you visions of heaven and other places and give you many revelations" (p 10-11). After her special assignment Mary K. Baxter published A *Divine Revelation of Hell* so all people can be warned of the reality of hell.

Twenty-two years later on Nov. 23, 1998, a dedicated Christian realtor was chosen for the same special assignment. At 3:00 a.m. Bill Wiese was hurled through the air and found himself naked and in a prison cell in hell. After 23 minutes of experiencing the horrible reality of Hell, Bill saw a burst of light which became Jesus. Relieved, Bill asked the Lord why he was sent to Hell. The Lord answered: "Because many people do not believe that hell truly exists. Even some of My own people do not believe that hell is real...Go and tell them about this place. It is not My desire that any should go there. Hell was made for the devil and his angels" (p 35). Bill followed the Lord's instruction and began telling his experience to others. In 2006 Bill wrote *23 Minutes in Hell* (Charisma House). The Lord reminded Bill that if a demon ever manifested to him, "All you have to do is cast them out in My name." The other instruction the Lord gave for Bill: "Tell them that I am coming very, very soon" (p 36). Praise the Lord for His mercy in forewarning us by the visitations to Hell of Mary K. Baxter and Bill Wiese.

Jesus said "Behold, I stand at the door and knock." and "My sheep hear my voice." (Jn 10:27). "See that ye refuse not Him that speaketh" (Heb 12:25). "Resist the devil, and he will flee from you.

Draw night to God, and He will draw nigh to you" (James 4:7-8). "...believe not every spirit, but try the spirits whether they are of God; because many false prophets are gone out into the world" (John 4:1). "Quench not the Spirit. Despise not prophesying. Prove all things; hold fast that which is good" (Ist Thess. 5:19-21).

THE STEPS OF OPENING OUR DOOR:

"Draw nigh to God, and He will draw nigh to you." James 4:8

During our years of broadcasting *The Christ at the Door Ministry*, one listener wrote: "It would be of great comfort if Jesus would visit us. I was always told it was a demon impersonating Jesus if anyone saw Him." Another listener wrote that her church implied that it wasn't good to seek an experience with the Lord. She truly hungered and thirsted for a visitation from the Lord but she didn't know how to open her door so the Lord could visit.

There are steps to opening our door to the Lord to let Him know we very much wish He would visit us. The first step in opening our door is the event of accepting Jesus Christ as our Lord and savior. Paul tells us, "That if thou shalt confess with thy mouth the Lord Jesus, and shalt believe in thine heart that God hath raised him from the dead, thou shalt be saved" (Rom 10:9). This is the event of salvation. Paul also tells us, "Wherefore, my beloved, as ye have always obeyed, not as in my presence only, but now much more in my absence, work out your own salvation with fear and trembling" (Phil 2:12). "Examine yourselves, whether ye be in the faith; prove your own selves. Know ye not your own selves, how that Jesus Christ is in you, except ye be reprobates?" (2nd Cor 13:5). This is the process of working out our salvation, examining ourselves to see if we are taking up our cross and following the Lord. Sara F. Adams, the author of the hymn *Nearer my God to Thee*

Draw night to God, and He will draw nigh to you" (James 4:7-8). "...believe not every spirit, but try the spirits whether they are of God; because many false prophets are gone out into the world" (John 4:1). "Quench not the Spirit. Despise not prophesying. Prove all things; hold fast that which is good" (Ist Thess. 5:19-21).

THE STEPS OF OPENING OUR DOOR:

"Draw nigh to God, and He will draw nigh to you." James 4:8

During our years of broadcasting *The Christ at the Door Ministry*, one listener wrote: "It would be of great comfort if Jesus would visit us. I was always told it was a demon impersonating Jesus if anyone saw Him." Another listener wrote that her church implied that it wasn't good to seek an experience with the Lord. She truly hungered and thirsted for a visitation from the Lord but she didn't know how to open her door so the Lord could visit.

There are steps to opening our door to the Lord to let Him know we very much wish He would visit us. The first step in opening our door is the event of accepting Jesus Christ as our Lord and savior. Paul tells us, "That if thou shalt confess with thy mouth the Lord Jesus, and shalt believe in thine heart that God hath raised him from the dead, thou shalt be saved" (Rom 10:9). This is the event of salvation. Paul also tells us, "Wherefore, my beloved, as ye have always obeyed, not as in my presence only, but now much more in my absence, work out your own salvation with fear and trembling" (Phil 2:12). "Examine yourselves, whether ye be in the faith; prove your own selves. Know ye not your own selves, how that Jesus Christ is in you, except ye be reprobates?" (2nd Cor 13:5). This is the process of working out our salvation, examining ourselves to see if we are taking up our cross and following the Lord. Sara F. Adams, the author of the hymn *Nearer my God to Thee* knew this process for in the third stanza she wrote: "There let the way appear, Steps unto heav'n." These steps are given in the Bible. We can rightly divide the "word of truth" to find these steps (2nd Tim 2:15).

Jesus summarized this process when He said, "As many as I love, I rebuke and chasten: be zealous therefore, and repent. Behold, I stand at the door and knock. If any man hear my voice, and open the door, I will come in to him, and will sup with him, and he with me."

In an earlier chapter we told the visitation experience of Dr. A. Stanley Rogers, the founder of the Christ at the door ministry. His visitation was a rebuke. Stanley worked and prayed step by step until he achieved a communing relationship with the Lord. Step by step Stanley opened his door to the Lord Jesus Christ. We are privileged to share the steps the Lord revealed to Stanley with you.

The first step is called "to His feet." We come to the feet of Jesus to repent in humility. This is the step Jesus gave when He said, "As many as I love, I rebuke and chasten: be zealous therefore and repent." Jesus demonstrated this step of humility by washing the feet of his disciples at the last supper. Jesus said, "I have set you an example that you should do as I have done for you. I tell you the truth, no servant is greater than his master, nor is a messenger greater than the one who sent him. Now that you know these things, you will be blessed if you do them" (Jn 13: 15-17). The prodigal son repented and returned to his father, humbled by the mistakes he had made. The Bible gives two examples of women who literally came to the feet of Jesus. First, " a certain woman, whose young daughter had an unclean spirit, heard of Him, and came and fell at His feet" (Mark 7:25). She approached the Lord in humility and her daughter was healed. Second, "When a woman who had lived a sinful life in that town learned that Jesus was eating at the Pharisee's house, she brought an alabaster jar of perfume, and as she stood behind him at his feet weeping, she began to wet his feet with her tears. Then she wiped them with her hair, kissed them and poured perfume on them" (Luke 7: 37,38). She came to the feet of Jesus and her sins were forgiven.

The December 1971 *Guideposts* gave the testimony of a flight captain who before each flight prays, "Lord, I thank You again for making it possible for me to do what I love most—fly this plane. Be with us, please, on this flight. I am nothing without You." The flight captain said, "I don't know quite how to explain it, but there is something totally reassuring and powerful that comes through those five words, 'I am nothing without You.' Whenever I say them—and I have thousands of times—it's as though there is fulfillment of His promise, 'Lo, I am with you always, even unto the end of the world.'" The first step in opening our door to His visitation is to come to His feet in repentance and humility.

The second step of opening our door to the Lord is called "to His heart." In this step we experience God's love for us and the forgiveness of our sins; we are taken to His heart. The beatitudes tell us "Blessed are the pure in heart: for they shall see God" (Matt 5:8). The disciple John leaned on Jesus' bosom at the last supper (Jn. 13:23). "For the eyes of the Lord run to and fro throughout the whole earth, to shew himself strong in the behalf of them whose heart is perfect toward him" (2nd Chron 16:9). The hymnist Harry D. Clark in 1924 wrote about this step: "Into my heart, into my heart, come into my heart, Lord Jesus; come in today, come in to stay, come into my heart, Lord Jesus."

The third step of opening our door to the Lord is the step of "in His name." We learn to serve the Lord. Jesus spoke of this step when He said "...He that taketh not his cross and followeth after me, is not worthy of Me" (Mt 10:37). As we take up our cross and start to serve the Lord we learn how to rightly use the power of His name. Jesus sent the seventy disciples out two by two to learn how to serve in this step of "In His Name." Luke 10:17 says, "And the seventy returned again with joy, saying, Lord, even the devils are subject unto us through thy name." The key to this step is to realize the power is in the name of Jesus; we have no power of our own. Another key is to use this power only when directed by the Lord. Jesus warns that the power of His name can be used wrongly; only those that use the power of His name as directed by Him are His disciples. "Many will say to me in that day, Lord, Lord, have we not prophesied in thy name? And in thy name have cast out devils? And in thy name done many wonderful works? And then will I profess unto them, I never knew you: depart from me, ye that work iniquity" (Matt 7:21-23). When by prayer we ask for something we end our prayer, "In Jesus' name."

When a lame man at the Beautiful gate of the temple asked Peter for alms, Peter replied, "Silver and gold have I none; but such as I have give thee: In the name of Jesus Christ of Nazareth rise up and walk." Peter pointed out to the assembled crowd that it was not his own power or holiness that healed the lame man; it was the power of God; and Peter preached to all those assembled.

The next step of opening our door to the Lord that He may enter into our lives is "In the shadow of His wings." David said, "How excellent is thy loving kindness, O God! Therefore the children of men put their trust under the shadow of Thy wings" (Psalm 36:7). "Be merciful unto me, O God, be merciful unto me; for my soul trusteth in thee; yea, in the shadow of thy wings will I make my refuge, until these calamities be overpast" (Psalm 57:1). "Because thou hast been my help, therefore in the shadow of thy wings will I rejoice" (Psalm 63:7).

In this step notice David says, "in the shadow of thy wings will I make my refuge, until these calamities be overpast." In other words, the nearness we felt to the Lord at conversion seems to have diminished. We are on our own, but under the shadow of the wings of the Lord we know He watches over us if we can just have faith. In the early 1400s Thomas A. Kempis wrote about this step in *The Imitation of Christ*. "Many love Jesus so long as no adversities befall them. Many praise and bless him, so long as they receive any consolations from Him. But if Jesus hide himself, and leave them but a little while, they fall either into complaining, or into too much dejection of mind. But they who love Jesus for the sake of Jesus, and not for some special comfort of their own, bless Him in all tribulation and anguish of heart, as well as in the highest comfort." In this step calamity might befall us, and we may feel the Lord has departed, but it only seems that way. If we can be steadfast in our faith that He is with us, we are under the shadow of His wings.

The next step of opening our door to the Lord is to move from being in the shadow of His wings to being directly "under His wing." We move from serving in remembrance of Him to serving in His Presence. We now know that Christ is with us. The psalmists wrote of this step. "...in the shadow of thy wings will I make my refuge..." (Psalm 57:1). "He shall cover thee with his feathers, and under his wings shall thou trust: his truth shall be thy shield and buckler" (Psalm 91:4). "I long to dwell in your tent forever and take refuge in the shelter of your wings" (Psalm 61:4). God's nation of Israel originally had the protection of this step of being "under His wings." Two cherubims stretched forth their wings and covered the mercy seat and the ark of the testimony. But Israel lost the privilege of being in the shelter of His wings. Jesus tried to restore Israel to the step of "under His wings." Matthew 23:37 says, "O Jerusalem, Jerusalem, thou that killest the prophets, and stonest them which are sent unto thee, how often would I have gathered thy children together, even as a hen gathereth her chickens under her wings, and ye would not!"

A famous Christian classic is *The Practice of the Presence of God* by Brother Lawrence. His letters were to bring his readers to this step of the shelter of His wings. "Were I a preacher, I should, above all other things, preach the practice of the presence of God" (5th letter). When we can feel the presence of God we are under the shelter of His wings.

The next step of opening our door to the Lord is to serve in the "shelter of the rock". We find a safe harbor for a season. The psalmists were familiar with this step. "For who is God save the Lord? Or who is a rock save our God. It is God that girdeth me with strength, and maketh my way perfect" (Psalm 18:31,32). "Unto thee will I cry, O Lord my rock; be not silent to me: lest if thou be silent to me, I become like them that go down into the pit" (Psalm 28:1). "Truly my soul waiteth upon God: from Him cometh my salvation. He only is my rock and my salvation; He is my defense: I shall not be greatly moved" (Psalm 62: 1, 2). "The Lord liveth; and blessed be my rock; and exalted be the God of the rock of my salvation" (2nd Samuel 22:47). Peter wrote of Christ being the chief corner stone, the rock of our faith (1st Peter 2:1-9). Hymnist Augustus Toplady wrote of this step: "Rock of Ages, cleft for me, Let me hide myself in thee." In the 23rd Psalm David gave thanks for the shelter of the rock: "Yea, though I walk through the valley of the shadow of death, I will fear no evil: for thou art with me; thy rod and thy staff they comfort me. Thou preparest a table before me in the presence of mine enemies. Thou anointest my head with oil; My cup runneth over. Surely goodness and mercy shall follow me all the days of my life: and I will dwell in the house of the Lord for ever" (Psalm 23:4-6).

"Serving in His Stead" is the next step of closeness to the Lord; the next step of opening our door to the fullness of Jesus Christ. "And of his fullness have all we received, and grace for grace" (Jn: 1:16). "Till we all come in the unity of the faith, and of the knowledge of the Son of God unto a perfect man, unto the measure of the stature of the fullness of Christ" (Ephesians 4:13). Elihu came in God's stead to Job saying, "Behold, I am according to thy wish in God's stead" (Job 33:6). The value of being in God's stead: "If there be a messenger with him, an interpreter, one among a thousand, to shew unto man his uprightness. Then he is gracious unto him, and saith, Deliver him from going down to the pit: I have found a ransom. His flesh shall be fresher than a child's: he shall return to the days of his youth: He shall pray unto God, and he will be favourable unto him: and he shall see his face with joy: for he will render unto man his righteousness" (Job 33:23-26). Paul came in God's stead to the Corinthian church: "we pray you in Christ's stead, be ye reconciled to God" (2nd Cor 5:20).

Moses reached this step because God could speak directly with Moses and Moses in turn was an interpreter for God to Israel. Rachel asked her husband Jacob for a child, but Jacob answered, "Am I in God's stead?" Jacob was saying, I haven't reached the goal of being an interpreter for God; I am not in God's stead. I can't help you (Gen 30:1-2). But God was merciful and hearkened to Rachel and God himself opened her womb and she conceived (Gen 30: 22-23). A listener to our broadcasts wrote to us stating that she was in church listening to her minister preach as usual. But this Sunday morning she saw the

Lord appear behind the minister. She knew the minister was in God's stead that morning with a message from God just for her needs.

The final step in opening the door to our heart, our home, our entire lives to the Lord is to walk with Him "in His presence." John 14:18-21 says, "I will not leave you comfortless: I will come to you. Yet a little while, and the world seeth me no more; but ye see me: because I live, ye shall live also. At that day ye shall know that I am in my Father, and ye in me, and I in you. He that hath my commandments, and keepeth them, he it is that loveth me: and he that loveth me shall be loved of my Father, and I will love him, and will manifest myself to him."

The final step is the blessing of walking daily with the Lord. We know the Lord because we are in His presence. We have the privilege of walking in the white robes of purity (Rev. 3:5). We have the privilege of the Lord teaching us about God: "For I have given unto them the words which thou gavest me" (John 17:8). We have the privilege of becoming more like the Lord: "I in them, and thou in me, that they may be made perfect in one" (John 17:23). We have the blessing of partaking with the Lord of the hidden manna: "To him that overcometh will I give to eat of the hidden manna..." (Rev 2:17). "I am the living bread which came down from heaven" (John 6:51). Our fellowship with the Lord lets us partake of the hidden mysteries in God: "That they all may be one; as thou, Father, art in me, and I in thee, that they also may be one in us" (John 17: 21). Finally we are privileged to sit with the Lord in His Father's kingdom. "To him that overcometh will I grant to sit with me in my throne, even as I also overcame, and am set down with my Father in his throne" (Rev 3:21). "And this is life eternal, that they might know thee the only true God, and Jesus Christ whom thou hast sent" (Jn 17:3). "And this is the will of him that sent me, that every one which seeth the Son, and believeth on him, may have everlasting life: and I will raise him up at the last day" (Jn 6:40).

Yes, step by step we can open our door to the Lord until we have the blessing of supping with Him and He with us.

The Steps of Discipleship

*A*part of most NDEs is the life review. The dying person is shown a rapid review of their entire life – the good and the bad. Paul told the members of the Galatian church to do a spiritual life review. In 2 Cor 13:5 he says, "Examine yourselves, whether ye be in the faith; prove your own selves. Know ye not your own selves, how that Jesus Christ is in you, except ye be reprobates?" We can open our door to our Lord and invite Him into our heart, life and home step by step. After the experience of salvation, the Lord tells us to take up our cross and follow Him. He calls us to be His disciples in our modern day just as he called twelve disciples two thousand years ago. These steps of discipleship are mentioned in the Bible.

The Lord revealed the following steps of discipleship to Dr. A. Stanley Rogers as his prayer life deepened over the years. These steps are another part of the theology of A. Stanley Rogers whose Christian life started when the Lord called him by bodily appearing on the running board of his Marmon car in Kansas City, Missouri, to rebuke him for his lifestyle shortly before the Great Depression. These steps are to help you open your door to your Lord Jesus Christ.

The first step of becoming a disciple of the Lord is to respond to our call; to answer His call. Romans 11:29 explains that the gifts and calling of God are without repentance. Jesus said He came not to call the righteous, but sinners to repentance (Mk 2:17). The gifts and calling of

God are without repentance, but His call should lead to repentance and accepting Jesus as our Lord and Savior.

The Bible tells of some remarkable calls. Moses was called when he looked at a bush that was burning but not consumed, and God audibly called, "Moses; Moses." And Moses answered, "Here am I." Samuel was audibly called but thought it was Eli the high priest calling him. Samuel finally answered, "Speak Lord, for thy servant heareth." Isaiah testified that "The Lord hath called me from the womb" (49:1). God called Isaiah a second time asking, "Whom shall I send, and who will go for us?" And Isaiah replied, "Here am I; send me" (6:8). Good examples of how to respond to our call.

The gifts and calling of God are without repentance. Many times sinners call to God in desperation to start their walk with Christ. People can become a prisoner to the earth by being a prisoner to alcohol, drugs, gambling, etc. They ask the Lord to make them His prisoner to free them from sin. Paul was converted by being told what he must do as he was walking towards Damascus one day. So Paul wrote to the Ephesians, "I Paul, the prisoner of Jesus Christ" (3:1). Again (4:1) Paul writes: "I therefore, the prisoner of the Lord, beseech you that ye walk worthy of the vocation wherewith ye are called." Exchanging being a prisoner to sins of the flesh to being a prisoner of the Lord is a first step in answering the call to the Lord to take up our cross and follow Him as His disciple.

We are all familiar with the story of Bill W. Bill was a prisoner of alcohol and finally in desperation called out to God. His prayer: "If there is a God, let him show himself! I am ready to do anything." God answered Bill's call by first lighting up the room with a great white light, indicating His presence. Second, God indicated His presence as a wind of spirit. And finally, God indicated His presence by the peace Bill said he suddenly felt. He changed from being a prisoner to alcohol to being a prisoner of the Lord. Paul explains Bill W's predicament: (Rom 7:18-24) "So I find this law at work: when I want to do good, evil is right there with me. For in my inner being I delight in

God's law; but I see another law at work in the members of my body, waging war against the law of my mind and making me a prisoner of the law of sin at work within my members. What a wretched man I am! Who will rescue me from this body of death?"

Jesus answers: "As many as I love, I rebuke and chasten. Be zealous therefore and repent" (Rev 3:20). The hymnist wrote, "Jesus calls us, o'er the tumult of our life's wild, restless sea. Day by day His sweet voice soundeth, saying Christian, follow me." The prodigal son is an example of responding to the call of the Lord. The prodigal said, "I will arise and return to my Father." We also have to use our will to respond to God's call, either directly or through being called by another such as an evangelist, minister or priest calling in the Lord's stead

After receiving our call to follow the Lord as one of His disciples, the second step of discipleship is to answer God's call; to make our calling and election sure. Peter writes (2nd Peter 1:10-11): "Therefore, my brethren, be all the more eager to make your calling and election sure. For if you do these things, you will never fall, and you will receive a rich welcome into the eternal kingdom of our Lord and Savior Jesus Christ." A common way to make our calling and election sure is to be baptized or to join a church or in some way make a commitment to the Christian life. Jesus, you remember, was baptized by John and immediately Jesus was led by the spirit into the wilderness to be tempted of the devil (Mt. 3:13-4:1). Jesus made his calling and election sure by rejecting the devil's temptations for forty days and nights. We have to make a similar effort to not backslide into our former sinful way of life. To use the illustration of Bill W, Bill found that even though he had the experience of the Lord manifesting as light and wind rescuing him from the power of alcohol, he would still have to fight the urge to return to drinking. When the urge to have a drink overwhelmed him, he found that being able to talk to a recovered alcoholic helped him to overcome the urge to return to drinking. And Alcoholic Anonymous was developed to help other alcoholics make their calling to a life of sobriety sure.

The hymn "I Would Be True" gives us the way to make our calling and election sure in verse three. "I would be prayer-ful thru each busy moment. I would be con-stant-ly in touch with God; I would be tuned to hear His slightest whisper; I would have faith to keep the path Christ trod." Galatians 1:17-18 tells us that Paul went to the deserts of Arabia for three years, which was his period to make his calling and election sure before he started his ministry. Students go to seminary and study to make their calling to the ministry sure before they are ordained. So we all have to make our calling and election sure by taking up our cross and following the Lord. Our cross is simply to overcome our earthy, sinful, egoistic appetites. We invite the Lord to be ruler of our lives. We strive to love the Lord with all our heart, mind and soul, and to love our neighbor as ourselves. Jesus said (Mt 20:15), "For many be called, but few chosen." Many are unable to make their calling and election sure. Paul wrote to the Ephesians (4:1): "I urge you to live a life worthy of the calling you have received."

The next step of discipleship in taking up our cross and following Jesus is to become a servant of God. We usually think of discipleship as being just one step: accepting Jesus as our Lord and savior. It is true that Paul wrote: "whosoever shall call upon the name of the Lord shall be saved (Rom 10:13). But Paul also wrote to the Phillipians (2:12): "work out your own salvation with fear and trembling." The Bible speaks of the servant grade of discipleship. James, chapter 1 verse one: "James, a servant of God, and of the Lord Jesus, to the twelve tribes which are scattered abroad, greeting." Second Peter, chapter 1, verse 1: "Simon Peter, a servant and an apostle of Jesus Christ." The book of Jude, verse 1 and 2: "Jude, the servant of Jesus Christ, and brother of James, to them that are sanctified by God the father, and preserved in Jesus Christ, and called, mercy unto you, and peace, and love, be multiplied." Titus, chapter 1, verse 1: "Paul, a servant of God, and an apostle of Jesus Christ."

Jesus emphasized the importance of being a servant of God at the Passover Feast. After the meal Jesus took off His outer clothing and wrapped a towel around His waist, poured water into a basin and washed His disciples' feet and then dried them with a towel. Jesus dressed and returned to his place and addressed His disciples (Jn 13:12-16): "Do you understand what I have done for you. You call me teacher and Lord, and rightly so, for that is what I am. Now that I, your Lord and Teacher, have washed your feet, you should wash one another's feet. I have set you an example that you should do as I have done for you. I tell you the truth, no servant is greater than his master, nor is a messenger greater than the one who sent him. Now that you know these things, you will be blessed if you do them." Jesus demonstrated the importance of being a servant of God. In Matthew 20:27-28 Jesus again emphasizes the importance of being a servant: "and whosoever will be chief among you, let him be your servant, even as the son of man came not to be ministered unto, but to minister, and to give his life a ransom for many."

The next step of discipleship is to be pronounced a good and faithful servant. We remember the parable of the talents. The master entrusted different sums of money to different servants before he left on a journey. We remember one servant did not do a good job and the master pronounced him a wicked and lazy servant. But the other two servants who did a good job the master pronounced: "Well done, good and faithful servant. You have been faithful with a few things; I will put you in charge of many things. Come and share your master's happiness." Jesus also demonstrated this grade of being a good and faithful servant (Jn 4:34). Jesus said, "I can of mine own self do nothing; as I hear, I judge: and my judgment is just; because I seek not mine own will, but the will of the Father which hath sent me." On another occasion Jesus declared: "the words that I speak unto you I speak not of Myself; but the Father that dwelleth in Me, He doeth the works" (Jn 14:10). The good and faithful servant then is one who seeks to do the will of his master instead of his own will. The key to being a good and faithful servant is to do as Jesus did: "I seek not mine own will, but the will of the Father which hath sent me." Jesus said, "Not every one that saith unto me, Lord, Lord, shall enter into the kingdom of heaven; but he that doeth the will of my Father which is in heaven."

Jesus was teaching one day when a woman in the crowd called out to him, "Blessed is the mother who gave you birth and nursed you. " But Jesus replied: "Blessed rather are those who hear the word of God and obey it" (Lk 11:27-28).

The tasks to be a good and faithful servant: first, have a communing relationship in which God can tell us His will; second, obey and do the job the Lord gives us. Then we can share our master's happiness. Jesus emphasizes the point of starting with knowing His will first (Matt 7:21-23). "Many will say to me in that day, Lord, Lord, have we not prophesied in thy name? And in thy name (remember the grade of "in His name" as we work to open our door and invite the Lord into our life?) done many wonderful works? And then will I profess unto them, I never knew you: Depart from me, ye that work iniquity."

The next step of discipleship is to advance from being a good and faithful servant to being privileged to be called a friend of God. The gospel of John (15:13-17) records Jesus speaking of this grade of discipleship. "Greater love hath no man than this, that a man lay down his life for his friends. Ye are my friends, if ye do whatsoever I command you. Henceforth I call you not servants; for the servant knoweth not what his Lord doeth; but I have called you friends: for all things that I have heard of my Father I have made known unto you. Ye have not chosen me, but I have chosen you, and ordained you, that ye should go and bring forth fruit, and that your fruit should remain; that whatsoever ye shall ask of the Father in my name, He may give it you. These things I command you, that ye love one another."

So the privilege in this grade is fellowship with the Lord. "Ye are my friends, if ye do whatsoever I command you." A good and faithful servant also wants to know the master's will before he does it – not in his way but in God's way. But the blessing is that a friend of God has a more intimate communion with God that God can give him the reasons for His instructions. The Lord can explain the whys and whereof of His plan.

The Bible gives examples of disciples who attained the grade of friends of God. Jesus pronounced his disciples His friends. Moses was a friend of God. Exodus 33:11: "And the Lord spake unto Moses face to face, as a man speaketh unto his friend." James 2:23: "Abraham believed God, and it was imputed unto him for righteousness; and he was called the Friend of God." Second Chronicles 20:7: "…Abraham thy friend for ever." Isaiah 41:8: "But thou, Israel, art my servant, Jacob whom I have chosen, the seed of Abraham my friend." Notice the mention of the two grades of discipleship: servant and friend.

The next step of discipleship is the privilege of being called "son of man." The Lord pronounces the disciple his son or his daughter. To be called a faithful servant of God is a privilege; to be called a friend of the most high is a greater privilege, and to be called a son or daughter of the most high is to be considered "family." (Ezekiel 2:1): "Son of man, stand upon thy feet, and I will speak unto thee. And the spirit entered into me when he spake unto me, and set me upon my feet, that I heard him that spake unto me. And he said unto me, Son of man, I send thee to the children of Israel, to a rebellious nation that hath rebelled against me: they and their fathers have transgressed against me, even unto this very day." God uses this term "son of man" over eighty times to Ezekiel. Daniel was also pronounced a son of man (8:17). After Daniel had been given a vision, the angel Gabriel was told to help Daniel understand the vision. Gabriel said, "Understand, O son of man: for at the time of the end shall be the vision." You can see the blessings from God and the fellowship with God that Ezekiel and Daniel enjoyed in this grade of discipleship.

A Christian lady in her testimony didn't realize she had reached this high grade of fellowship. She had accepted the Lord as her Lord and Savior at an early age. She grew in her faith as a child. Her dream was to go to a Bible College after high school. She worked after school to save for college. The summer before college her father became ill and was unable to work. Family finances became depleted and her father asked if he could use her college savings to keep the family going. Of course she gave her father her college savings. But how could she go to college? She prayed to know what to do. One day the Lord spoke to her in a voice she heard audibly. The Lord said, "Daughter, you go ahead. I'll see you through." And He did.

The final step of discipleship is to progress from a 'son of man' to being a 'son of God.' Paul said that salvation is both the event of accepting Jesus Christ as our Lord and Savior (Rom 10:13) and also the process of "work out your own salvation with fear and trembling. For it is God which worketh in you both to will and to do of His good pleasure. Do all things without murmuring and disputing: That ye may be blameless and harmless, the sons of God, without rebuke, in the midst of a crooked and perverse nation, among whom ye shine as lights in the world, holding forth the word of life" (Phil 2:12-15). The goal is to work until we can be a son of God. Jesus is *The* son of God, but calls us to be a son of God. John starts his gospel by explaining that Jesus "came unto His own, and His own receive Him not. But as many as received Him, to them gave He power to become the sons of God, even to them that believe on His name: Which were born, not of blood, nor of the will of the flesh, nor of the will of man, but of God (Jn 1:11-13). The first epistle of John 3:1-3: "Behold, what manner of love the Father hath bestowed upon us, that we should be called the sons of God; therefore the world knoweth us not, because it knew Him not. Beloved, now are we the sons of God, and it doth not yet appear what we shall be: but we know that, when he shall appear, we shall be like Him, for we shall see Him as He is. And every man that hath this hope in him purifieth himself, even as He is pure."

Paul (Rom 8:13-17): "if ye live after the flesh, ye shall die; but if ye through the Spirit do mortify the deeds of the body ye shall live. For as many as are led by the Spirit of God, they are the sons of God."

Gal 4:4-7: "God sent forth His son, made of a woman, made under the law, to redeem them that were under the law, that we might receive the adoption of sons. And because ye are sons, God hath sent forth the spirit of His son into your hearts, crying, Abba, Father. Wherefore thou art no more a servant, but a son; and if a son, then an heir of God through Christ." The Psalmist (82:6): "I have said, Ye are gods; and all of you are children of the most High." When, in John 10:31-42, the Jews attempted to stone Jesus because he said he was the Son of God, He reminded them that they were all to be sons of God. Because He went to prepare a place for us, by His power, and by His overshadowing we can all become His disciples and step by step strive to be sons of the living God. He is right at our door, calling us to be His disciples. If we follow Him step by step we can become sons of the living God. St. Irenaeus stated that God became a human being in order that human beings might become God.

David E. Taylor in *My Trip to Heaven: Face to Face with Jesus* (2011, Destiny Image) gives similar steps of discipleship, which the Lord revealed to David. We will summarize these steps, which David explains in detail. First is the disciple relationship with Jesus; second, the servanthood relationship with Jesus. Third, sonship with the Lord; fourth, the marriage covenant with God; fifth, the love covenant relationship with the Lord; sixth, the covenant of the right hand relationship with the Lord, and seventh, the covenant relationship with Jehovah God the Father. The Lord explained to David the importance of working out our salvation in fear and trembling: "There's a difference in My kingdom with those who love me. Everyone who is a believer is not necessarily part of the elect or married to Me in this level of union. There is a difference in relationship levels with Me. I will be as close and intimate as you will allow Me to be. Like in the natural realm, there is a difference between friendship, sonship, servanthood, stewardship, kingship, and the marriage relationship" (p 172).

We thank Dr. A. Stanley Rogers and David E. Taylor for their closeness to God that they might share guideposts to help us love the Lord so much that we wish to take up our cross and follow Him until we are privileged to be sons of God in a covenant relationship with Jehovah God the Father.

The Mind of Christ

Paul said to the Christians at Philippi, "Let this mind be in you, which was also in Christ Jesus" (Phil 2:5). To the Romans (11:34) Paul asked, "For who hath known the mind of the Lord? Or who hath been his counselor?" Later Paul adds (Rom 12:2), "And be not conformed to this world: but be ye transformed by the renewing of your mind, that ye may prove what is that good, and acceptable, and perfect, will of God." To the Corinthians Paul asked (2:16), "For who hath known the mind of the Lord, that he may instruct him?" Then Paul answers his own questions saying, "But we have the mind of Christ."

Jesus in Rev 3:20 gives us a challenge: "If any man hear my voice and open the door, I will come in and sup with him and he with me." In other words we have the opportunity to live with the Lord daily. There is a way of life, deep hid in God through Christ. Jesus says, "My sheep hear My voice…" (Jn. 10:27). Jesus visits us and if we invite Him into our lives we can make His visitation a continuous walk through life by walking with Him daily. We can learn to let Him visit our mind so we can align our minds with Him. The Bible calls this "being in the mind of Christ." There are many ways Jesus can visit us awake and asleep. He can visit us bodily and He can also visit us mind to mind.

Alexander Loyd, PhD, ND, tells us his mind visitation in his book *The Healing Code* (2010, Grand Central Life & Style). Alexander's wife, Tracy, was clinically depressed and she came from a family with clinical depression so bad that seven members of her family had committed suicide in the last thirty years. For twelve years Alexander had tried everything to help his wife's depression. In fact Alexander had studied the mental health field and searched his way through two doctoral programs in search of help for his wife. In addition he had attended seminars and read books in search for a solution. He became a professional therapist as well as a minister. In 2001 he was attending another seminar looking for answers and was in the airport on his way home when he received a call from his wife on his cell phone. She was so severely depressed that she was weeping and calling for help. After praying with his wife, Alexander received a message from the Lord, mind to mind. Alexander said, "God downloaded into my mind and heart what we now call *The Healing Codes*" (p 4). He said the experience was unlike any he had ever experienced. God was depositing into his head a blueprint of a healing system he had never studied. As this blueprint was deposited into his mind he started writing it down. As God revealed the system to him he wrote as fast as he could until he finally said, "God, you're either going to have to slow down or remind me of this; I can't write that fast."

A physical mechanism of using simple exercises with the hands plus prayer was revealed to counteract the true sources of all life's issues. When he got home, he instructed his wife to use the blueprint God had revealed and in 45 minutes his wife's clinical depression was gone. A miracle. The following day he started using the blueprint God revealed for his patients' mental and emotional problems. Eight years later, he shared God's revelation for us all in his book *The Healing Code*. After years of study and prayer, God revealed a way of healing mind to mind to Alexander we can all use.

In the written Word of God, James 5:14-15 has a healing code for sickness: let the elders of the church pray and anoint the sick with oil in the name of the Lord. Second Peter 1:12 tells us to be established in the present truth. Alexander Loyd's healing code was given by the

Living Word of God for our present day and the advantage is that it can be prayed and used by the individual himself. The Lord can direct us which prayer and healing method to use – from the Written Word of God or from the Living Word of God - or to use both.

Paul may have been referring to our ability to receive mind to mind from God by the ability some have called intuition. We think of Einstein as having a great mind – a great rational mind. But Einstein said, "I did not arrive at my understanding of the fundamental laws of the universe through my rational mind." Einstein was referring to our ability to receive from the Mind of God when he said, "The most beautiful experience we can appreciate is the sensation of the mystical...He to whom the emotion is a stranger, who can no longer wonder and stand in awe is as good as dead." Even in theology our seminaries stress rational thinking rather than seeking to develop our intuitive ability. We need to heed Einstein's advice: "We shall require a substantially new manner of thinking if mankind is even to survive."

Alexander Lloyd had a visitation experience mind to mind. Paul said in Romans 12:2, "...be ye transformed by the renewing of your mind." When God speaks to us mind to mind we are transformed. Socrates, the famous Greek philosopher, openly said that God had given him a gift to hear God's voice mind to mind. The philosopher Nietzsche stated that one becomes nothing but a medium for super-mighty influences. That which happens can only be termed revelation. Nietzsche received revelation from God mind to mind. A survey of natural scientists made by the American Chemical Society found that 83 percent realized that their solutions came not from their rational mind but by a flash of insight which we recognize as coming from the Mind of God. The 83 percent said that when they faced a problem, they would have an unpredictable flash of insight which would illuminate the essentials of a solution to their problem with obvious adequacy and finality. A similar questionnaire sent to mathematicians found that intuition and faith were also the foundation for their math solutions. The mathematicians said that deductive and inductive reasoning were later used as the superstructure built upon the foundation of the revelation they were given. Mathematician Gaus said he had struggled with a mathematical theorem for many years using his rational mind with no results. He said his solution came not on account of his painful efforts, but by the grace of God. "Like a sudden flash of lightening the riddle happened to be solved." Even a questionnaire sent to American inventors also found that their inventions were based upon a flash of insight which we call the "Mind of Christ" or the "Mind of God".

Scientist John S. Mill stated, "The truths known by intuition are the original premises from which all others are inferred." Research scientist and engineer R. Buckminster Fuller in his book *No More Secondhand God* (1967, Southern University of Illinois Press) also talks about a future time he foresees when we will need no intermediaries but we will all be able to contact God directly mind to mind. Fuller is referring to Rev 21:3: "Behold, the tabernacle of God is with men, and He will dwell with them, and they shall be His people, and God himself shall be with them, and be their God."

If you want to know God's will for a problem in your life, how can you contact the Mind of Christ? We suggest a three step method. First start by using the scientific method; use your physical senses to investigate and collect the material facts about your situation or problem. Second, study the problem with your logical, rational mind. Think through the problem. Finally, and most important, pray and use your intuitive mind to receive the solution the Lord has for you. The old advice to "sleep on it" gives the Lord the additional help of dreams to instruct us. Elihu's advice to Job can help us understand why "sleeping on it" can help. "For God speaketh once, yea twice, yet man perceiveth it not. In a dream, in a vision of the night, when deep sleep falleth upon men, in slumberings upon the bed; Then he openeth the ears of men, and sealeth their instruction" (Job 33:14-16).

Another practical way to know the mind of Christ is given by Lew Miller in his 1977 book *Your Divine Connection* (1977, Celestial Arts). Lew suggests to envision your mind as a miniature theater. By prayer first and then relaxation Lew instructs the reader how to receive from the Lord, mind to mind. Lew says that if we think of our mind as a movie screen we can visualize the Lord's solution as He flashes it on the mind's screen. Lew's technique is an application of the Lord's command in Mark 11:24: "What things soever ye desire, when ye pray, believe that ye receive them, and ye shall have them." Jesus demonstrated this relationship with His father. Jesus said, "the words that I speak unto you I speak not of myself: but the Father that dwelleth in me, he doeth the works" (John 14:10). The relationship Jesus had with His father, we can have with the Lord. Paul said, "Let this mind be in you, which was also in Christ Jesus" (Ph 2:5); "...walk not as other Gentiles walk, in the vanity of their mind" (Eph 4:17), and "...be renewed in the spirit of your mind" (Eph 4:23).

Metapsychiatrists are scientists who do not use the term "mind of Christ," but are looking at the capacity of the mind to receive exceptional kinds of knowledge and awareness through channels that are not known at present. Edgar Mitchell, a former Apollo 14 Astronaut and the first director of The Institute of Noetic Sciences, believes that the attainment of an ennobling level of consciousness is not a mere philosophical speculation, but is needed for the realization of man's potential as a total human being and may even be necessary for man's ultimate survival as a species on the planet earth.

Psychiatrist Stanley R. Dean in *Psychiatry and Mysticism* (1975, Nelson Hall) doesn't use the term "the mind of Christ"; instead he speaks about the ultraconscious summit. "The full ultraconscious summit, though rare, produces a superhuman transmutation of consciousness that defies description. The mind, divinely intoxicated, literally reels and trips over itself, groping and struggling for words of sufficient exaltation and grandeur to portray the transcendental vision. As yet we have no adequate words....The individual is bathed in emotions of supercharged joy, rapture, triumph, grandeur, reverential awe, and wonder....An intellectual illumination occurs that is quite impossible to describe."

The ultraconscious summit during a NDE (near death experience) is not rare at all, but occurs in many NDEs. The mind of the NDEr is changed by coming into the presence of the Lord. Dr. Kenneth Ring in *Heading Toward Omega: In Search of the Meaning of the Near-Death Experience* (1985, Harper Perennial) tells of Tom's experience. Tom had been an undistinguished student in high school and didn't even like to read. When Tom was 33 years old he briefly died when he was working underneath his truck and it fell on him. Tom was in the presence of God as light. "The light communicates to you and for the first time in your life…is a feeling of true, pure love….The second most magnificent experience…is you realize that you are suddenly in communication with absolute, total knowledge…you can think of a question…and immediately know the answer to it. As simple as that….Upon entering that light….the atmosphere, the energy, it's total pure energy, it's total knowledge, its total love, pure love—everything about it is definitely the afterlife, if you will." Tom had a new mind as the result of his NDE.

Jesus Christ is at the door of your mind. Paul tells us in Eph. 4:23-24: "…be renewed in the spirit of your mind; and…put on the new man, which after God is created in righteousness and true holiness." One of the founders of psycho-somatic medicine, Dr. Franz Alexander tells us: "The fact that the mind rules the body is, in spite of its neglect by biology and medicine, the most fundamental fact which we know about the process of life." The famous psychologist William James said, "The greatest discovery of my generation is that human beings, by changing the inner attitudes of their minds, can change the outer aspects of their lives."

Paula Rinehart in *Strong Women – Soft Hearts* (2001, Thomas Nelson) tells the mind visitation experience of her lawyer friend, Bob. Bob was spending a morning with the Lord in prayer. Bob said to the Lord, "I need to know, Lord, if you really love me." Bob said that as clear as a bell he heard: "Well, Bob, what do you think?" Bob sat for a moment and then he replied, "You're right, Lord. You do love me. I know you love me."

Your prayer time can include a quiet time so Jesus Christ can visit you by speaking to you mind to mind.

The Visitations of Paul, Thomas Aquinas, and Ramond Llull

Paul's visitation on the way to Damascus is well known to Christians. In chapter 9 the author of Acts gives the details of Paul's visitation: Paul was surrounded by a heavenly light and then heard the Lord ask him: "Saul, Saul, why persecutes thou me?" In Acts, chapter 22, Paul tells how the first visitation of the Lord changed his life instantly as he preached to a multitude in Jerusalem. In Chapter 26 Paul again tells how his first visitation resulted in his conversion as he appeared before Agrippa. His testimony caused the king to say, "Almost thou persuadest me to be a Christian." The first visitation of the Lord to Paul on the road to Damascus has been called a turning-point in the history of Christianity. But this was just the first visitation of Paul.

Acts 23:11 tells of another visitation in which the Lord bodily visited Paul during the night and stood by Paul to encourage Him. When the Lord visits us there is always an uplift to our entire being, which is the result of the love and power that He brings. Finally 2nd Corinthians 12:1-4 records another majestic and possibly the final visitation of Paul when he was "caught up to the third heaven." In the paradise of this visitation Paul heard unspeakable words "which it is not lawful for a man to utter." Paul did not boast of this visitation, rather he spoke of his infirmities. In summary, Paul's ministry began with a majestic visitation on earth; visitations directed his earthly ministry but a majestic heavenly visitation sealed his ministry. For a similar progression from earthly to heavenly visitation and the dramatic change in behavior visitations bring, let's look at the visitations of another great Christian, Thomas Aquinas.

Thomas Aquinas (1225-1275) is one of only 35 Doctors of the Catholic Church. He was pronounced a saint in 1323 by Pope John XXII. His theology is held in high esteem by the Catholic Church and entire Christendom. As a theologian his life's work had been to reconcile Greek philosophical humanism with Judeo-Christian revelation. He had been composing the *Summa Theologiae*, which was the masterpiece of his life's work. On December 6, 1273, he was celebrating Mass in the chapel of St. Nicholas. Biographers say that during the Mass he was "strangely disturbed." In hindsight we know Thomas had a majestic heavenly visitation.

As a result of this heavenly visitation, Thomas stopped working on the Summa in the middle of the third part of the Tract of Penance. His co-worker Brother Reginald finally compelled Thomas to confide his reason for suddenly abandoning his work. Thomas told him, "Everything I have written seems to me like so much straw compared to the truths which I have seen, and which have been revealed to me. Brother Reginald, the end of my work has come, and I hope that the end of my life will come as soon as the end of my teaching." His prayer was answered and his health rapidly declined and he died soon after his heavenly visitation. He did no more theological writing after this heavenly visitation and left the completion of his Summa to others. We wish Thomas had shared with us the insights he received from his heavenly visitation.

Let's look at the earlier visitations of Thomas Aquinas which can help us prepare for our visitations. His final heavenly visitation was not a sudden "bolt from the blue." It was the final chapter of a life of devotion and earlier visitations from the Lord. Let's look at how his earlier life prepared him for his final grand visitation.

Born into a wealthy family, at age five his parents vowed him to the local Benedictine monastery of Monte Cassino. He scorned his family wishes for plans to head a local rich feudal monastery and instead he pursued a life of service as a Mendicant Religious. As he advanced to prominence in theological circles, his spiritual life was his foundation. Biographers said that before writing he always began work by kneeling in prayer to ask for enlightenment. A revelation from the Lord gave him the subject of the text of his doctoral thesis. He daily practiced prayer and contemplation and as a result he had ecstasies, visions and revelations. Biographers wrote that He was visited by two angels when he resisted the temptation of a prostitute who was hired by his family to try and dissuade him from joining the Dominican order when he was nineteen. Several times the Lord visited and spoke to him audibly, saying: "You have written well of me, Thomas." One biographer wrote that when Christ spoke and confirmed his teaching he was not only in ecstasy but was elevated from the floor. Biographers say he had visions of the Virgin Mary, St. Paul and St. Peter.

Let's compare the visitation experiences of Paul and Aquinas. Paul was a Jew and was active in persecuting Christians. But on the road to Damascus the Lord's visitation caused such a sudden insight and understanding that Paul changed the course of his thinking, as well as his motive for living. Before the visitation, Paul was a Jew in good standing and was so opposed to Christianity that he persecuted Christians. The Lord's visitation caused an abrupt change in Paul's living and thinking. Aquinas in contrast, was a devout Christian and prayed for insight before he wrote. Even so, the Lord's visitation to Aquinas allowed him to see such splendor that his thinking was not so much reversed as elevated to so high a level that Thomas didn't want to return to his previous level of inspiration. During his life Thomas prayed daily that his theology be what the Lord desired. And the Lord visited and approved of what he wrote several times. But the heavenly visitation of the Lord ushered in truths of such a higher dimension that Thomas saw the contrast immediately. He was so humbled by that contrast between what he had written even with the Lord's inspiration and what the Lord directly revealed that he quit his earthly writings and prepared to join the Lord in heaven.

For a third example of how a visitation of the Lord can immediately change our life, let's look at the life of Ramon Llull (1232-1315). Ramon was born into a wealthy family and by 1257 had married and had two children. He had a good life as a tutor to James II of Aragon and later was the administrative head of the royal household to the future King James II of Majorea. But he also lived a licentious and wasteful life as a troubador. He had a natural ability to compose licentious songs and poems.

In 1263 during the evening he was in the process of starting to sing a vulgar song when his attention was directed to his right. He saw the Lord Jesus Christ on the cross suspended in mid-air. This visitation vision came five times to him. This visitation of the Lord brought the power and love to transform Ramon's life. Ramon left his family, his royal position, and entered into a nine year period of study which resulted in his becoming a member of the Third order of St. Francis. His life now had purpose. He had three goals: 1. to die in service to God; 2. to found religious institutions that would teach foreign languages to its students; 3. write a book that would overcome objections to converting to Christianity. In 1274 divine revelation gave him his method of logic which was finally published in 1290: *The Abbreviated Art of Finding Truth*.

So instead of composing vulgar songs, his life's work was to use logical means to produce knowledge. Today's computer scientists affirm that his system of logic was the beginning of information science. He was interested in converting Muslims to Christianity and made missions from Spain to Africa. His method of conversion was by prayer and conversation instead of by military force. During his last mission in 1314 he was stoned by Muslims for his efforts and died the following year. He is honored as a martyr by the Franciscan Order and was beautified by Pope Paul IX in 1847. Ramon Llull University was founded in 1990 in Barcelona, Spain.

Paul gave his final testimony saying, "For I am now ready to be offered, and the time of my departure is at hand. I have fought a good fight, I have finished my course, I have kept the faith: Henceforth there is laid up for me a crown of righteousness, which the Lord, the righteous judge, shall give me at that day: and not to me only, but unto all them also that love his appearing"(2nd Timothy 4:6-8). Thomas Aquinas and Ramon Llull, also loved His appearing. By recognizing God's plan of visitation we can all learn how to prepare for His appearing – His visitation. For He promises to appear to all men, women and children when He said: "Behold, I stand at the door and knock."

Visitation and Nations

We recognize that the nation of Israel was started by visitations from God. The Bible starts with the story of the creation of Adam and Eve and then the visit of God to Adam and Eve in the garden. The sons of Adam walked with God and generations later Noah continued the walk with God. God said that with Noah, he would establish his covenant (Gen 6:18). Many generations later God visited Abram and guided Abram in his travels until at another visitation God changed his name to Abraham and said, "for a father of many nations have I made thee" (Gen 17:5-6). Genesis tells the story of the visits of God to Abraham's children as the nation of Israel began. Jacob's visitation by dream included a ladder from earth to heaven with angels of God ascending and descending (Gen 28:12-17). Visitations continued to the generations of the new nation. As Joseph was dying he prophesied: "God will surely visit you, and bring you out of this land unto the land which He sware to Abraham, to Isaac, and to Jacob" (Gen 50:24-25). Moses' visitation by the angel of the Lord at the burning bush continued God's growth of the nation of Israel (Ex 3).

God called Moses to come to Him at Mt. Sinai and God manifested as a thick cloud before Israel "that the people may hear when I speak with thee, and believe thee for ever" (Ex 19:9). God first asked Moses with Aaron, Nadab and Abihu and seventy of the elders of Israel to worship him from afar. But later God invited the seventy plus

Moses, Aaron, Nada and Abihu to come close to Him. The scriptures are explicit that "they saw the God of Israel: and there was under his feet as it were a paved work of a sapphire stone, and as it were the body of heaven in his clearness. And upon the nobles of the children of Israel he laid not his hand: also they saw God, and did eat and drink" (Ex 24:10, 11). Notice the scriptures are explicit that even though they saw God "He laid not his hand." They were invited to see God and live. The fact that man can see God and live is reflected in Jesus invitation in Revelation 3:20 that He wishes to be invited into our abode so He can again be seen and we are privileged to fellowship and live daily with Him.

We can see another fact about God's plan of visitation in the story of the rebellion of Korah, Dathan and Abiram. They didn't believe that God had chosen Moses to be the leader of Israel. Their argument was that the entire congregation was holy. Wasn't the Lord equally among them all? Moses arranged a way for Israel to "know that the Lord hath sent me to do all these works; for I have not done them of mine own mind. If these men die the common death of all men, or if they be visited after the visitation of all men; then the Lord hath not sent me" (Num 16:28, 29). We recall that those in rebellion didn't die the death of all men; the earth swallowed them up and they died an uncommon death. Also they had not yet been visited after the visitation of all men. True, they were part of a holy congregation as they maintained, but if they had received their individual visitation, their contact with God at their visitation would have brought the understanding why God chose Moses as their leader and they would not have been jealous of the leadership of Moses. This story is important because it tells us that God's plan is to visit every man, woman and child in some way in their lifetime.

Why does God have a plan to visit all his children at least once in every lifetime? Acts 10:34 explains that God is no respecter of persons. He loves all His creation equally, whether they be great or small, rich or poor, famous or common. Romans 11:29 explains that the gifts and calling of God are without repentance. So God's plan of visitation is to call His children to Him regardless of whether they have lived a righteous or sinful life. In fact His calling can call us to repentance so we can have the blessing of fellowship with Him.

Later in the history of the nation of Israel, after the nation had turned from following God, the prophets warned of the coming day of visitation. Isaiah asked (10:3): "...what will ye do in the day of visitation?" Hosea prophesied (9:7): "The days of visitation are come..." Jeremiah warned (51:18): "...in the time of their visitation they shall perish."

Jesus spoke of His coming as a visitation to the nation of Israel (Lk 19: 42-44). Jesus wept over Jerusalem saying, "If thou hadst known, even thou, at least in this thy day, the things which belong unto thy peace! But now they are hid from thine eyes. For the days shall come upon thee, that thine enemies shall cast a trench about thee, and compass thee round, and keep thee in on every side, and shall lay thee even with the ground, and thy children within thee; and they shall not leave thee one stone upon another; because thou knewest not the time of thy visitation."

The nation of Israel was the result of visitations of God to their first leaders. When Israel turned from a direct walk with Him, God next visited Israel through prophets who attempted to call the nation back to a daily walk with Him. Finally God sent His Son to visit His nation and call the nation back to His Presence. And Jesus could only weep when Israel did not recognize Him. He was the sacrifice to reunite all mankind to God. Next, the Lord visited Paul who extended God's plan of salvation from just the nation of Israel to all the gentile nations.

For another national visitation, let's go to the 1400s in Europe during the Hundred Years' War between France and England which was 75 years old. France was torn between the rule of the Duke of Burgandy, who was an ally of the English, and the rule of young Dauphin Charles who was the heir to the throne of France but had not yet been crowned. In 1424, twelve year old Joan of Arc was in the garden of her peasant parent's home when a dazzling light shone by her right hand. Joan of course was terrified until from the midst of the glory of the light a voice congratulated her for her faith and her observance of her faith. The voice then gave her a mission; she was to seek the uncrowned King of France, rescue him and crown him King at Reims. After her commission was given the third time she saw the source of her heavenly voice. She saw the Archangel Michael in his splendor and around Prince Michael she saw the solders of Heaven. Joan said she saw her angelic visitors "with the eyes of my body, as plainly as I see you now; and when they went away, I would cry. For I wanted them to take me with them." The angel visitors returned to her every two or three days, week after week urging her to fulfill the mission God had given her. Her devotion to God grew and after three years she obeyed her commission. And we are familiar with the rest of her story. A visitation to a young girl to rescue and guide a nation.

For our next visitation to a nation, let's go to Philadelphia on July 4, 1776. Delegates of all the colonies had drafted the declaration of independence after hours of debate in the State House. They met in the lower chamber with doors locked and a guard posted because they knew signing such a declaration would mean the death penalty for high treason. All the delegates had "talked the talk" but were unwilling to "walk the walk." They were all talking about how they would surely die by axes, scaffolds, and the gibbet if they signed because the King of England would kill them for treason.

Suddenly an unknown speaker spoke up in a strong bold voice. Here is the Speech of the Unknown: "Gibbet! They may stretch our necks on all the gibbets in the land; they may turn every rock into a scaffold; every tree into a gallows; every home into a grave, and yet the words of that parchment can never die! They may pour our blood on a thousand scaffolds, and yet from every drop that dyes the axe a new champion of freedom will spring in to birth! The British King may blot out the stars of God from the sky, but he cannot blot out

His words written on that parchment there. The works of God may perish; His words never! The words of this declaration will live in the world long after our bones are dust. To the mechanic in his workshop they will speak hope: to the slave in the mines, freedom; but to the coward kings, these words will speak in tones of warning they cannot choose but hear. Sign that parchment! Sign, if the next moment the gibbet's rope is about your neck! Sign, if the next minute this hall rings with the clash of falling axes! Sign, by all your hopes in life or death, as men, as husbands, as fathers, brothers, sign your names to the parchment, or be accursed forever! Sign, and not only for yourselves, but for all ages, for that parchment will be the text book of freedom, the bible of the rights of man forever. Nay, do not start and whisper with surprise! It is truth, your own hearts witness it; God proclaims it. Look at this strange band of exiles and outcasts, suddenly transformed into a people; a handful of men, weak in arms, but mighty in God like faith: Nay, look at your recent achievements, your Bunker Hill, your Lexington, and then tell me, if you can that God has not given America to be free! It is not given to our poor human intellect to climb to the skies, and to pierce the Council of the Almighty One. But methinks I stand among the awful clouds which veil the brightness of Jehovah's throne. Methinks I see the recording Angel come trembling up to the throne and speak his dread message. 'Father, the old world is baptized in blood. Father, look with one glance of Thine eternal eye, and behold evermore that terrible sight, man trodden beneath the oppressor's feet, nations lost in blood, murder, and superstition, walking hand in hand over the graves of the victims, and not a single voice of hope to man.' He stands there, the Angel, trembling with the record of human guilt. But hark! The voice of God speaks from out the awful cloud: 'Let there be light again! Tell my people, the poor, and oppressed, to go out from the old world, from oppression and blood, and built my altar in the new.' As I live, my friends, I believe that to be His voice! Yes, were my soul trembling on the verge of eternity, were this hand frequent to death, were this voice choking in the last struggle, I would still, with the last impulse of that soul, with the last wave of that hand, with the last gasp of that voice, implore you to remember this truth—God has given America to be free! Yes, as I stare into the gloomy shadows of the grave, with my last faint whisper I would beg you to sign that parchment for the sake of those millions whose very breath is now hushed in intense expectation as they look up to you for the awful words: 'You are free.'"

The unknown speaker then walked over to the declaration and was the first to sign his name. The other delegates, inspired by the unknown speaker's oratory and example of signing, rushed forward to add their signatures. After all had signed, they wanted to express their gratitude to the unknown speaker who spoke with such divine authority, but he had suddenly disappeared. None of the delegates recognized him. Wanting to know who the unknown speaker was, they went to the declaration to see his signature. His signature would identify him. But now there was only a blank space above John Hancock's name who was the second to sign. And the blank space above John Hancock's name is seen to this day on the Declaration of Independence.

Who was the unknown visitor? Esoteric circles believe it was Saint Germain, one of the agents of the secret order guarding and directing the destiny of America. But could it have been Jesus Christ visiting in disguise to help start the New JerUSAlem? The scriptures report that several times when Jesus was preaching, his audience was so incensed at his message that they sought to kill him, but Jesus had the ability to suddenly pass through the midst of them (Luke: 4:30). Another time his audience was so angry that they took up stones to kill him "but Jesus hid himself, and went out of the temple, going through the midst of them, and so passed by" (John 8:59). Yet another time Jesus was accused of blasphemy for his teaching and the leaders sought to take him, "but he escaped out of their hand" (John 10:39). So we know Jesus or a messenger He sent had the power to manifest and by his speech bring the power the delegates needed to put their lives on the line for a declaration to benefit all of mankind.

Matthew Paul Turner fully develops the premise that America has a God-given mission in his (2014, Jericho Books) *Our Great Big American God: A Short History of our Ever-growing Deity*. Twenty thousand Puritans came to America seeking freedom of worship. In 1630 John Winthrop, a Puritan lawyer, was elected governor of the Massachusetts Bay Company. He proclaimed: "We shall be as a city upon a hill (and) the eyes of all people are upon us." Turner notes (p 24), "That America would become God's shining example to the world of how society and religion should coexist has been a narrative threaded throughout our nation's history. John Winthrop's vision of a 'city upon a hill' has become one of America's unofficial mottos." Note how President Washington in his Inaugural Address of 1789 carries forth this idea (p 87): "No people can be bound to acknowledge and adore the Invisible Hand which conducts the affairs of men more than the people of the United States. Every step by which they have advanced to the character of an independent nation seems to have been distinguished by some token of providential agency."

After reporting on the history of the great diversity of religion in America, Turner notes (p 222): "Because here in the United States of America, our God is great, our God is big, and our God is always growing."

The last visitation to America we wish to note is rather a series of visitations of the Lord to Choo Thomas and is written in her *Heaven is So Real* (2003, Creation House Press). Choo was born in Korea but came to the United States with her family. Her family was not religious but before her mother became pregnant with Choo her mother dreamed that on a clear day sudden clouds formed in front of her house and then one cloud came into the room where she was sleeping and filed the room with a white glow. Choo became a Christian in 1992. She received the fire of the Holy Spirit while praying at home in 1994 and a month later first saw the Lord's presence while worshiping in her Tacoma, WA church. By 1995 Choo had a profound spiritual experience when her body began to shake violently. Two weeks later she received the gift of speaking in tongues while at home. She felt the anointing of God's Holy Spirit while watching a Benny Hinn crusade on TV. By January 1996 she had an expectancy in her heart and yearned to hear the Lord's voice. As she continued to mature in her religious life by mid-January, 1996, she heard the Lord say, "My daughter. Choo Nam, I am your Lord, and I want to talk to you."

The Lord began to visit Choo daily, showed Choo His presence at these visits, and gave her special spiritual gifts so she could fulfill His mission of being chosen an End-Time Prophetess. The Lord would waken her at night, take her out of her earthly body and in her spiritual body she would walk with the Lord to a beach. With the Lord she would walk to the entrance of a shiny tunnel, walk through the tunnel to the other side to another beach. From this beach they would fly through the air to heaven. Choo would be directed to a powder room by an angel who would put a gown and crown on her and then she would be able to worship the Lord before His throne. After being shown a part of heaven, Choo would return to the powder room where the angel would remove her heavenly attire and the Lord would accompany her to the spiritual beach, through the tunnel to the earthly beach and back to reunite with her body in bed.

Her mission: The Lord told her, "I want all My children to know that I am coming soon." Instead of giving all the details of the Lord's message through Choo for all Christians, we urge you to read *Heaven is So Real* because the Lord's visitation and His message for all the world through Choo is so important. On December 8, 1999 the Lord told Choo that "*Heaven is so Real* will be the last chance for people to realize how soon I am coming for My people. If the disobedient people don't wake up, they will not hear the trumpet sound, and they will have to go through the tribulation. I have been giving them many signs to bring prayer back into the schools, but people are not really trying to do it. I will never force anyone's mind. I can only give them signs so they will know what I want them to do. I have given enough warning for people to know what I want them to do for so long. I cannot wait forever for those who don't want to be ready for Me. I am coming for those who are ready for Me, and this will happen sooner than they expect."

What a blessing than a Korean American woman was chosen to be the End-Time prophetess of His Visitation to all nations.

VISITATION DURING SICKNESS:
Shelly Godfrey's testimony

*S*helly is a personal friend of Rose Miller and shared her amazing story of a God Visitation she had during a serious illness. This occurred while she lived in Las Vegas. She now lives in Prescott, Arizona.

On June 12, 2007, I went into the hospital for a routine hysterectomy. I was discharged the next day. My mother had come from Tucson to stay with me during my recovery. Around noon Saturday, June 16, I was still in so much pain that, even though I thought I was being a baby, Mom and I decided I should go back to the hospital. I told her it might be a good idea to call the ambulance.

The ambulance arrived in about 10 minutes. The last thing I remember is being put onto the gurney. I woke up almost a month later in ICU on life support. What happened during those weeks was revealed to me slowly by my husband, Lance and my friends and family.

When we arrived at the ER that Saturday the doctor could not figure out what was wrong with me. I didn't even have a temperature. He even sent my CAT scans to a friend of his to look at because he just didn't see anything. Since I had complained for several days that I could not go to the bathroom they decided they should try an enema. But the doctor kept looking at my records. He said I was just too sick; there had to be more. Moments before they were going to give me the enema, the doctor yelled at them to stop. He had finally seen the problem. I had a perforated colon and was in septic shock. The reason I didn't have a fever was that I was far beyond that.

I was rushed to surgery; (this was over 8 hours after I had come into the hospital). The surgeon later told me she believed I was going to be the first person who ever died on her table, and that I was already doing the "guppy breaths" when she got there. During surgery I had a heart attack, then another one a few days later.

For the next 16 days the doctors couldn't tell my husband if I was going to live or die. The consensus was my chances for survival were 1 in 100. Ten days after my first surgery the head surgeon and internist were arguing. One said I needed to be opened up again because the infection was winning and I would die without the surgery. They other said I couldn't handle another surgery and would die if they did it. They left it up to my husband to make that choice.

I have a prayer group of 7 other women that I had been a part of for many years. Our sole purpose for getting together weekly was to pray for each other. One of those women runs a Christian counseling center and had been one of my best friends for over 20 years. A client of hers was a head nurse at the hospital where I was a patient. My friend told her that I was in the hospital where she worked; the nurse said, oh yes, everyone knew about me. When my friend asked what she thought about my chances for recovery, the nurse just looked at her and said, "Pat, you're friend is not going to make it."

Sometime during that 16-day life and death teeter totter, I found myself at the light, and there beside me was my God. The God of creation, the God of the universe, chose to come beside me and speak to me. The first thing He said to me was, "you have believed rightly and you can come home." I was so excited. I had accepted Christ when I was in my 30's but had always had doubts. Was I believing in the right thing; did I believe enough, and on and on. I didn't trust my faith. What beautiful words: "you can come home." Oh yes, I want to come home. Then He said to me "But – "Don't you hate it when someone tells you "yes – but!" He said, "But if it were My will that you stay where you are, knowing I am with you and would protect you, would you be willing to do that?" Now, let me explain to you what He was asking me to do. At the light I had no memory of this world, my life, or anyone in it. Where I was, at the light, I sensed an evil surrounding me that to this day I can't put into human words. Think of the most horrible thing the world of cinema could conjure up and multiply that a hundredfold. It was unspeakable terror. This is where He was asking me if I was willing to stay. I have no idea if my decision took 5 minutes or the whole 16 days on the edge of death. I had to go into my innermost being to decide how much I trusted my God. I finally said, "Yes, if it is Your will, I would stay here." Then I woke up. I kept repeating two phrases that God had given me. *"There is one God, Creator of the universe"* and *"I am a daughter of the King."* I kept saying it over and over. One of my very good friends, a former surgical nurse, had been staying by my side with Lance for days. I would grab her and say, "And you are a daughter of the King." She needed to know. Of course, I didn't realize until later that no one could understand a word I was saying since I was on a ventilator.

I would learn later that during the time I was "gone" my husband, my good friends, and even some of the nurses, could sense an evil. They sensed there was a spiritual battle going on. But something else was happening while I was gone. There were literally thousands of prayers from all over the world going up on my behalf. During those prayers, there were things happening in the lives of many of those people that confirmed to them the goodness of God. I can't tell you of all the stories I continued to hear long after I was out of the hospital. Stories of how God was made so real and evident in all of this.

It took me a long time to process everything that was happening to me when I finally woke up. I remember being incredibly fearful for a time. Every time someone came to move me or take me for a test was a fearful experience. I remember crying out to God in my fear.

The Gospel of Visitation

The next time I was being wheeled down for another test, He gave me the most incredible vision. 2nd Kings 6:17 says: "and the Lord opened the servant's eyes and he looked and saw the hills full of horses and chariots of fire all around Elisha." That was the vision given to me. I was surrounded by an army of protection. I can still see thousands of mounted soldiers. In fact His vision was so explicit I even remember banners of turquoise flying around me. My fear was gone from that moment on.

When I finally went home, I was on fire to tell everyone about my experience. I couldn't keep quiet. My home health care nurse was the first one I grabbed and told my experience. When I was sent home the incision that they had made was left open, as it had to heal from the inside out. When the nurse looked at my incision she looked puzzled. She asked me when I had the surgery. When I told her she said, "Your incision is healing miraculously fast. It should take weeks for this to come this far and it's only been days."

I have come to understand that what happened to me wasn't about me at all. God still performs miracles today. My situation was hopeless. He used my body to show people that He is still in control and still answers prayers. My perk in all of this was that I got to meet the Living God one on one.

Today I am completely healthy. I'm on no medications and have no residual effects from everything I went through. God gives each of us a testimony. Our responsibility is to share what He has given us with others. I remember getting so frustrated when I would tell someone what happened to me and they would be less than impressed. Finally God told me very clearly that my job was to tell the story. How that person received the story and what happens later is none of my business, it's His.

What I can say confidently is this: There is a God. He is a personal God. The God of the universe takes time to stand by us and speak to each one of us. If that doesn't blow you away, I don't know what will.

Conclusion

The story of Jonah is a Christian classic. Jonah was given a job to do by the Lord. Jonah dilly dallied. But when Jonah was swallowed by the whale, Jonah knew God was serious. Do your job or else. So Jonah went to Ninevah as he had been told, preached and performed his commission from the Lord. The story of the Christ at the door ministry is another Jonah story. A. Stanley Rogers was visited when the Lord appeared at the door of his Marmon car in Kansas City and rebuked him for not tithing. Soon Stanley lost his wife, health and wealth as the Lord had predicted. He prayed and repented until during a mid-day nap an angel took him to heaven for another visitation. He was privileged to absorb so much love that he passed out and awoke to find his head on the Lord's breast. Stanley eventually remarried and found a co-worker who was known as "Mother Kathryn" by the White Light doctors.

Stanley and Mother Kathryn wanted a face to face relationship with the Lord. They contacted all the well-known mediums of the day with a proposition. You can contact "the other side." Why not use your talent to contact the Lord? Their answer? Yes, we can contact spirits; yes, the Lord lives in the spiritual realm, but we don't have the faith that we can contact the Lord. What to do? Stanley and Mother Kathryn had to learn how to pray and contact the Lord themselves. Their prayer life and daily walk with the Lord became a full time quest to know the Lord and His will and plan for their life. And later,

His will and plan not only for their lives and for the White Light doctors they taught and served, but also a quest to know the Lord's plan for His return at His Second Coming.

When Mother Kathryn was called to the other side by the Lord, her passing solidified Stanley's contact with the Lord because their close communion that had grown during their marriage on earth, now extended from heaven to earth. Stanley now had his own contact with God plus his contact with God through his wife. The priests of Israel could receive answers from the Lord by the jewels of the urim and thummim lighting to give a 'yes' or 'no' to questions asked by the priest who wore the breastplate of righteousness. David had his divining cup to also commune with the Lord. The thousand doctors Stanley had taught to enquire of the Lord concerning the healing of their patient's didn't realize the significance of the healing power that came from the Lord, but Stanley realized the Lord had a plan for his life.

Stanley's healing ministry ended when a thousand doctors had been taught to heal with the Lord's overshadowing at the radionic instrument. There were different groups of healers using the radionic instrument but white light radionics was the only group that asked the Lord's overshadowing, hence the name "white light radionics." There was a nucleus of white light doctors and laymen who gathered with Stanley to maintain their contact with the Lord. They gathered at what was known as the "Western Temple" to worship on Sundays when possible. Another group of white light doctors and laymen lived in Pennsylvania and gathered with Leland Wood and his family at what was known as the "Garden Spot." This group also gathered on Sundays to worship together when possible.

A third grouping of white light doctors formed in Elkhart, Indiana. Your author was a part of this nucleus which became known as "The New Acre." In the 1960s on his semi-annual missionary trip, Stanley brought the good news from the Lord that the communion with the Lord that white light doctors had been privileged to enjoy was to be shared with all of God's children. The good news was to be broadcast on radio that Jesus can be seen, felt, and known. The program was to be called The Christ at the Door Ministry, based upon the Lord's promise of Revelation 3:20. The radio ministry was not to ask for contributions. Was this just a private revelation to Stanley in the 1960s? No, the Lord confirmed his instruction by speaking twice. Stanley had transferred planes in Detroit and a Detroit paper carried the news item of the Lord visiting a boy preacher in rural West Virginia. The Lord's appearance at the church had started a revival.

Stanley's initial visitation experience progressed to a daily walk with the Lord: a habitation; a face to face relationship with the Lord. That is, he enjoyed daily visitation. Stanley knew the visitation experiences of the white light doctors. He knew of the book called *Love Can Open Prison Doors*, the visitation of Starr Daily. As we began the Christ at the Door Ministry on WKAM, Goshen, IN., we testified that Jesus truly was at the door by telling our own visitation experiences. As we began looking for the testimony of others who had Christ at the Door experiences, we read about Kathryn Kullman, Oral Roberts and other ministers and evangelists. As we read Guideposts and Full Gospel literature we noted other visitation stories which we used to help the listener realize that Jesus really is at the door in our modern age. Soon we became aware that visitation experiences were everywhere.

Guideposts began a sister publication which told of angel visitations. The Near Death Experiences of those who had a heavenly visitation became well known as books appeared to acquaint everyone with the ultimate visitation experience. Next we became aware of the experiences of those who were taken to heaven without dying. Roxanne Brant's ministry and other ministries solidified the promise of the Lord to visit his own. Our broadcasts followed a simple formula: Two of us would talk with the audience instead of preaching at the radio audience. We would give a Biblical example of visitation and then a modern day example of visitation to build the listener's faith that they too could have the joy of being visited in some way by the Lord.

Finally we found fellow travelers who were also helping build the faith that Jesus really is at our door. G. Scott Sparrow, Ed.D. published *I Am with You Always, True Stories of Encounters with Jesus; Sacred Encounters with Jesus; Witness to His Return, Personal Encounters with Christ;* and *Blessed Among Women, Encounters with Mary and Her Message.* We noted the Lord calling more disciples to proclaim the good news. Evangelist David E. Taylor in his books *My Trip to Heaven: Face to Face with Jesus* (2009) and *My Trip to Heaven: Face to Face with Jesus* (2011) also proclaims the good news that Jesus comes through our door to live with us daily if we just have the faith to invite Him in. The Lord has visited Choo Thomas (*Heaven is So Real*) as His end-time prophetess to alert us that His return is imminent.

Paul explained to the Corinthian church that he "planted" the good news of the gospel; his fellow servant Apollos "watered" his work, but it was God who gave the increase (1 Cor 3:4-11). We have mentioned just a few of the many who have been given a part of the great commission that He is openly appearing before He returns to the earth at His Second Coming. Because Jesus was crucified for the redemption of our sins, and because of His resurrection, He earned the right to return and visit His own; indeed to resurrect His Father's plan to visit His creation in the cool of the morning of each day.

The Christ at the Door Ministry has been privileged like Paul and Apollos to do a small part in proclaiming the good news: Jesus Christ is at your door. Won't you let Him into your life?

If you would like to share your story of visitation, feel free to contact us:

Dr. Hal Miller: halmiller@mtecom.net

Rose Miller: rosemiller@mtecom.net

Dr. Hal Miller
18100 N Las Vegas Road
Prescott, Arizona
86305

Christ at the Door Ministry
PO Box 436
Goshen, IN
46528

www.christatthedoor.com